ROB COUTEAU is a Brooklyn-born author and visual artist. His publications have been praised in *Evergreen Review*, *Publishers Weekly*, *New Art Examiner*, *Midwest Book Review*, and *Witty Partition*. In 1985 he won the North American Essay Award, sponsored by the American Humanist Association. His work has been cited in books such as *Ghetto Images in Twentieth-Century American Literature* by Tyrone Simpson, *Gabriel Garcia Marquez's 'Love in the Time of Cholera'* by Thomas Fahy, *Conversations with Ray Bradbury* edited by Steven Aggelis, and David Cohen's *Forgotten Millions*, a book about the homeless. His interviews include conversations with Pulitzer Prize-winning author Justin Kaplan, *Last Exit to Brooklyn* novelist Hubert Selby, Simon & Schuster editor Michael Korda, LSD discoverer Albert Hofmann, Picasso's model and muse Sylvette David, sci-fi author Ray Bradbury, film star and bibliophile Neil Pearson, and historian Philip Willan, author *Puppetmasters: The Political Use of Terrorism in Italy*. Couteau has appeared as a guest on Bob Barrett's *The Best of Our Knowledge* (WAMC), Len Osanic's *Black Op Radio*, and on *Monocle 24* in Europe. Since 2020 he has devoted himself to republishing annotated texts of important but forgotten authors such as Stanley Marks, Charles Beadle, and Francis Carco. In 2023 he published *Intimate Souvenirs*, a memoir featuring an Introduction by Robert Roper, author of *Nabokov in America: On the Road to Lolita* and *Now the Drum of War: Walt Whitman and His Brothers in the Civil War*.

In 1954 in Vallauris, France, a beautiful young woman named SYLVETTE DAVID befriended the century's greatest artist. She soon became the subject of over a hundred of Picasso's drawings, paintings, and sculptures (one towering thirty-six-feet high). After this life-changing encounter, Sylvette devoted her life to painting. In 2017 she published *I Was Sylvette*, a memoir co-authored with her daughter, the sculptor Isabel Coulton. Sylvette's latest series of watercolors, commissioned for this book, portray a blind art collector, Léon Angély, and his precocious guide, Joséphine, who unwittingly inspired Picasso's greatest engraving.

ALSO BY ROB COUTEAU

Fiction:

Doctor Pluss
Afterword by Jim Feast

Essays and Interviews:

Collected Couteau

More Collection Couteau
Introduction by James Dempsey

*Portraits from the Revolution: Interviews with the
Protestors from Occupy Wall Street*

Poetry:

The Sleeping Mermaid
Introduction by Christopher Sawyer-Lauçanno

Selected Poems
Introduction by Ed Foster

Memoir:

Intimate Souvenirs
Introduction by Robert Roper

Edited and Annotated by Rob Couteau
Dominantstar Publications

Charles Beadle:

*A Passionate Pilgrimage. Edited with an Introduction
and Afterword by Rob Couteau*
Postscript by John Locke

Dark Refuge.
Edited with Annotations and an Afterword by Rob Couteau
Postscript by Christopher Sawyer-Lauçanno

Francis Carco:

From Montmartre to the Latin Quarter.
Edited with Annotations and an Introduction by Rob Couteau
Afterword by Christopher Sawyer-Lauçanno

Stanley J Marks:

Murder Most Foul! The Conspiracy That Murdered President Kennedy:
Edited with an Introduction by Rob Couteau

Two Days of Infamy: November 22, 1963; September 28, 1964
Introduction by Rob Couteau

Coup d'Etat! Three Murders That Changed the Course of History.
President Kennedy, Reverend King, Senator R. F. Kennedy
Introduction by Rob Couteau

A Murder Most Foul! A Three-act Play about the JFK Assassination
Introduction by Rob Couteau
Afterword by James DiEugenio

Picasso, Modigliani,
and a Blind Man
Crazy for Color

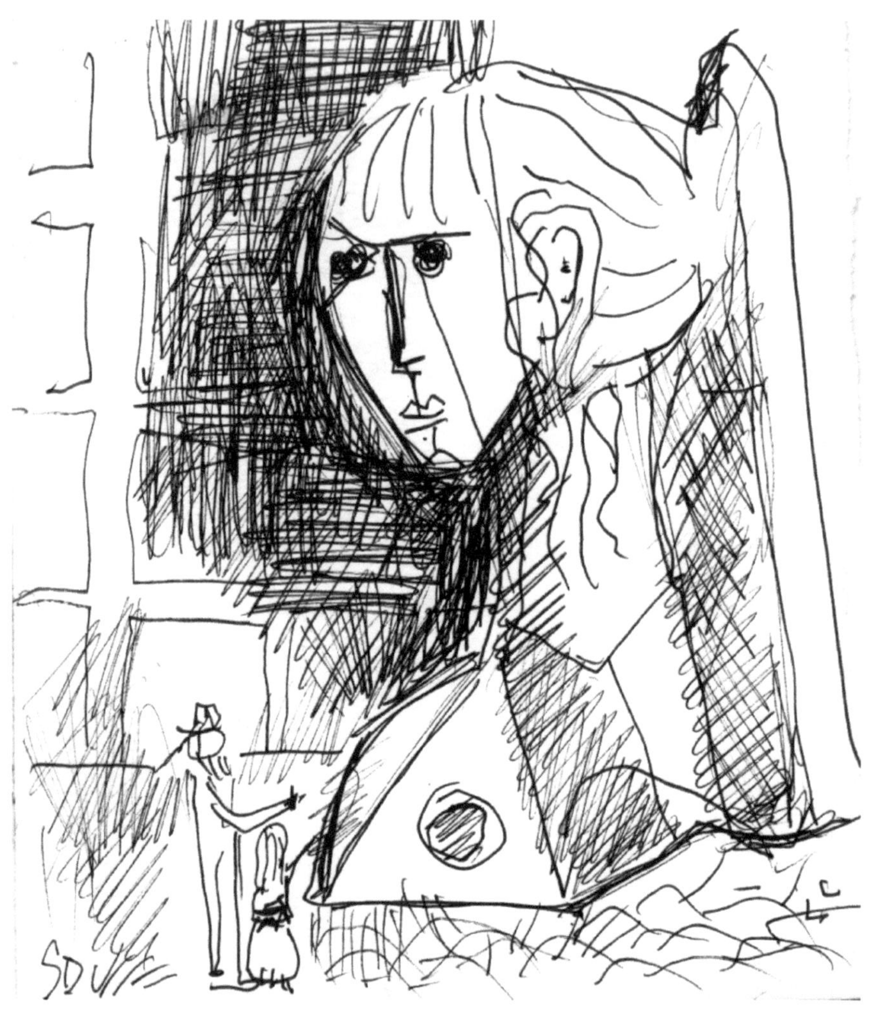

Sylvette David. *Le Père Angély and Joséphine Visit the Bust of Sylvette (II)*. Devon, England. December 2021. India ink on Langton watercolor paper, 8 ¼ x 6 ¾.

Picasso, Modigliani, and a Blind Man Crazy for Color

Illustrated by Picasso's Model and Muse, Sylvette David

A Tribute to Léon Angély
by Rob Couteau

Second, Revised Edition

DOMINANTSTAR

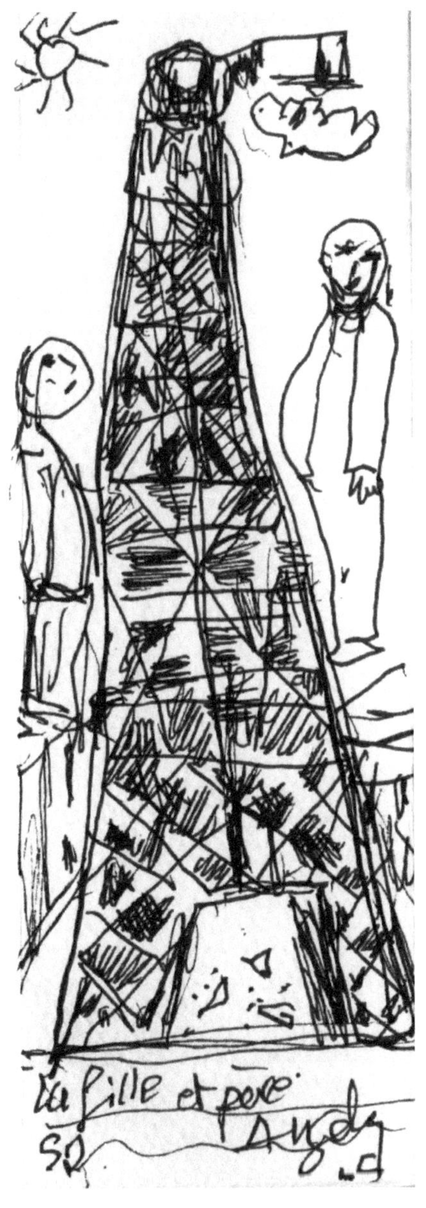

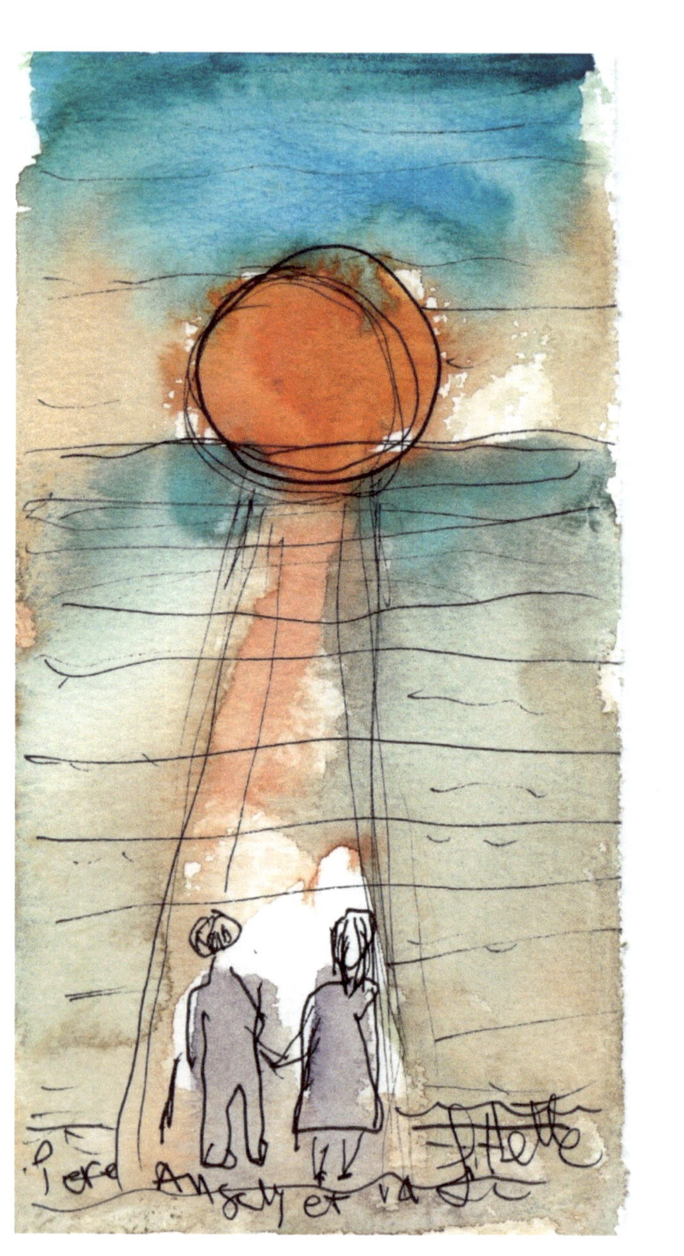
Pere Anselm et va fillette

Contents

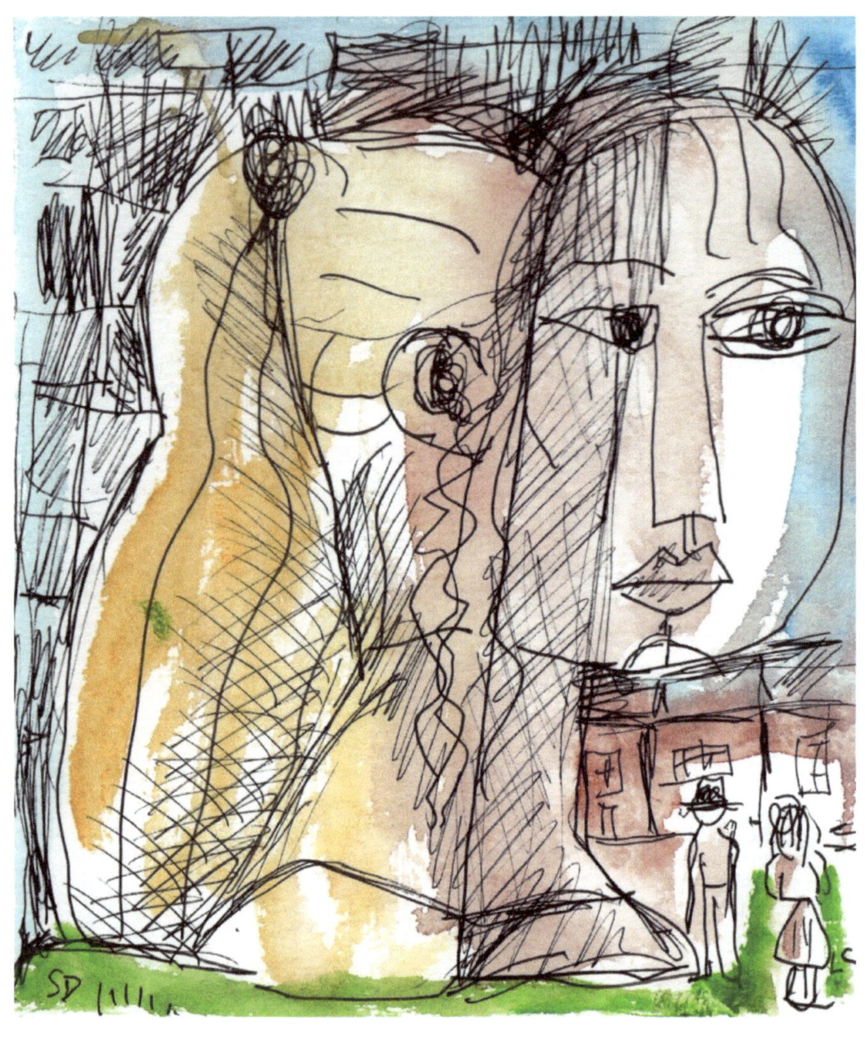

Sylvette David. *Le Père Angély and Joséphine Visit the Bust of Sylvette*. Devon, England. December 2021. Watercolor and India ink on Langton watercolor paper, 8 ¼ x 6 ¾ inches.

A Blind Man Crazy for Color

A turn-of-the-century art collector who was nearly blind. A girl who accompanied him on visits to Montmartre's ateliers and who served as his "eyes." The gradual accrual of a collection of what would later be hailed as modern masterworks, including Picassos, Utrillos, and Modiglianis. And the bitter fate of being forced to sell them for little more than they were originally purchased for, after the economy was rocked by World War I inflation … and just before prices in the art world skyrocketed. This is the story of Léon Angély – also known as "Père" Angély – and a mysterious gamine who may or may not have been named "Joséphine," about which so little is known.

Angély enters the art historical literature thanks to Charles Douglas' 1941 text, *Artist Quarter: Modigliani, Montmartre and Montparnasse*, in which the author writes that Modigliani once joked with the poet and journalist Louis Latourette: "Now I've only got one buyer and he's blind!"[1] Douglas continues:

This seemingly bitter joke was true. The buyer was one Père Angély, known on the Butte as Léon, a bald, fat little fellow who lived in an attic on the rue Gabrielle. He was a retired solicitor's clerk, myopic, who had collected pictures for years for such scanty prices as his small means afforded, and continued to do so on principle even when almost totally blind, in the hope of one day holding a sale by which he would realize enough to provide a comfortable income for his old age.

But he had to sell his collection of prospective "masters" for almost as little as he had given for them. The war intervened before his "stable" had acquired fame, and he died in 1921 as poor as Cousin Pons. [A reference to Balzac's *Le Cousin Pons*, from *Comédie humaine*.] Still, he outlived Modigliani. He was on the make, if you like, yet he had been a Good Samaritan to artists in their misery."[2]

A blurb in the original edition of *Artist Quarter* notes that Douglas was a habitué of Montmartre for thirty years and intimately acquainted with its denizens. Hence the book

> reveals the truth behind the many legends, is packed with authentic stories about writers and painters whose names are now household words, and contains much hitherto unpublished information about the life and career of Modigliani, obtained from his family and friends. Much of the text was written in Montmartre amid the scenes described, and after personal consultation with survivors of the great days when Frédé presided over the Lapin Agile and Libion, patron of the Café de la Rotonde, was beginning to rival him in Montparnasse.
>
> It is the most complete account which has yet been written in English of the birth of Cubism and other contemporary movements in modern painting, and of the lives and loves that started them.

Although the text reveals the "truth behind the many legends," the author's biography is itself semi-legendary. "Charles Douglas" is a portmanteau pseudonym of Douglas Goldring (1887—1960), a literary editor, poet, socialist journalist, and travel writer from Greenwich, England; and Charles Beadle (1881—?), a native of Hackney, London, who was born at sea and who published genre fiction and novels about Parisian bohemian life. (Most notably, a semi-autobiographical master-piece known as *Dark Refuge*.)

Goldring worked as an editor of literary magazines, publishing notable authors such as Ford Madox Ford and Wyndham Lewis. Because of his progressive views, he also had the honor of being ratted on by George Orwell, who added Goldring to his notorious list of writers who were supposedly Communist sympathizers, which eventually found its way to the Information Research Department of Great Britain's Foreign Office. Goldring was an outspoken libertarian and pacifist but never a Communist. He was also a poet, critic, and travel writer who spent the early Twenties on the French Riviera and in Paris, where it's possible that he encountered his future co-author.

Beadle was a world traveler who served in the British South African Police during the Boer War and who held various odd jobs in British East Africa, Uganda, Dutch Borneo, Morocco, the Congo, and the United States, where he frequently published genre fiction in magazines such as *Adventure*. He was acquainted with Modigliani while living in Paris during the 1910s and was the subject of one of his pencil drawings (circa 1915); settled in the City of Light for the long haul in the 1920s; and remained there until the looming threat of World War II forced him to return to England.[3] The date and circumstances of his death remain unknown.[4]

In *Artists Quarter* the narrator says that he became intimately acquainted with Modigliani around 1915, while living in Montmartre. Beadle's friend and neighbor, Beatrice Hastings, first met Modigliani the year before and became involved in a tempestuous relationship with the artist, which lasted from 1914 to 1916. "So it happened," continues the narrator, "that Modi came, for a time, to share this little retreat on the Butte, and he and I saw each other constantly."[5]

Therefore, it may have been from Modigliani himself that Beadle first heard about Léon Angély. (A character based upon Modigliani makes a few brief appearances in Beadle's 1928 satirical novel, *The Esquimau of Montparnasse*. Modi also plays a prominent role in Beadle's 1938 novel, *Dark Refuge*, where he appears as a thinly disguised fictional character named "Cecci.") Beadle's address at 7, place du Tertre, was located only a few blocks away from Angély's flat at 49, rue Gabrielle: a three-minute walk of about two-hundred meters.[6] Both locations were within walking distance of Picasso's Bateau Lavoir studio at 13, rue Ravignon, which intersects rue Gabrielle.

As we shall see while exploring the scant literature available on Angély, this brief paragraph about a blind visionary (which ends the eighth chapter of *Artist Quarter*, "Dealers of the Butte") will serve as a template for nearly everything written about him henceforth. But the authors of *Artists Quarter* fail to mention another crucial protagonist: a gamine who described the artwork to Angély, thus augmenting his physical and intuitive vision.

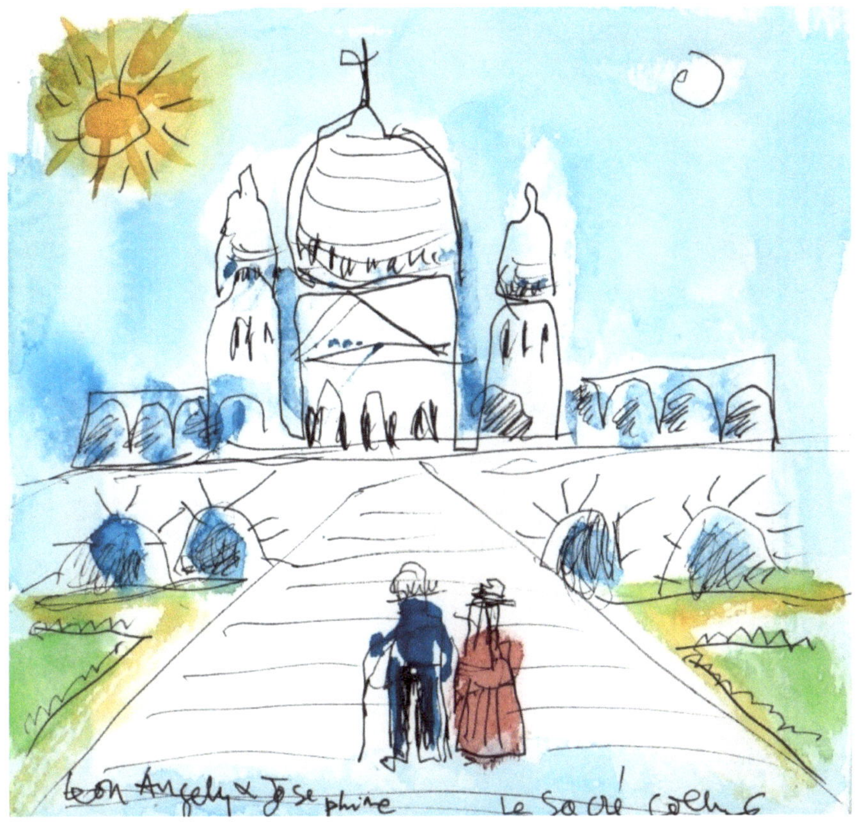

Sylvette David. ***Léon Angély and Joséphine, La Basilique du Sacré Cœur.*** **Devon, England. December 2021. Watercolor and India ink on Langton watercolor paper, 8 x 8 inches.**

Six years later, the story of Père Angély was portrayed in greater detail by the prolific French author Roland Dorgelès (1885–1973) in *Bouquet de Bohème* (1947). Dorgelès lived in the Bateau Lavoir[7] at the same time as Picasso and Braque, and he possessed firsthand knowledge of the Montmartre artist scene.

A World War I veteran, Dorgelès' novel about the war, *Les croix de bois* (Wooden Crosses; 1929), was later made into a motion picture directed by Raymond Bernard. Dorgelès was also known for his wry sense of humor. In 1910, after curators at the Louvre decided to cover the Mona Lisa with a sheet of glass, he mounted a one-man protest. Early one morning, he arrived at the museum with a straight-edged razor and proceeded to give himself a shave, using as a "mirror" the reflective glass that was mounted over a Rembrandt. (Decades later, such stunts would be labeled as "conceptual art," yet sadly enough they often lacked Dorgelès' acerbic sense of humor!)

Thanks to *Bouquet de Bohème* we learn that Léon collected the work of Pierre Dumont, a French painter who later became a Cubist and who lived in the Bateau Lavoir from 1910 to 1916. There, Dumont befriended artists such as Juan Gris, Max Jacob, and Apollinaire (all of whom were closely associated with Picasso). In a chapter bearing the witty title "Le destin est-il aveugle?" ("Is Fate Blind?"), Dorgelès cites Dumont as the source for the following information:

> Daily life thus offers us dramas that a novelist would hesitate to use: they are too well arranged. However, in stirring the memories of poor Dumont, I find an even more incredible detail: his first buyer in Montmartre was a blind man. A small annuitant with a few pennies, formerly an attorney's clerk, he was called Angély and lived on rue Gabrielle. His accommodation was cluttered with trinkets,

statuettes, and motley objects from the flea market [*Marché aux Puces*] to which he attributed a considerable value; and its four walls disappeared under the modern paintings that he'd purchased for ten francs each, which he considered to be so many masterpieces. When this mania had first seized him some twenty years earlier he could still see, and he chose his paintings with a very sure taste; but when he lost his sight his love of painting remained with him, and he continued to frequent the studios. Camped in front of an easel, leaning on his cane – head back, mouth half open – he listened attentively to the artist's description of the work and, suddenly, made up his mind, as if enlightened. Returning home, he stopped on the way to show his shopping, sometimes holding it backwards: "I chose well, eh? This is one of his best ..." And no one was flinching. In the evening, alone in his little museum, he dined on a meager soup cooked for him by the concierge, happier however than a billionaire surrounded by fake Chardins. He particularly liked canvases painted in full impasto, like those of Dumont. "The sky ... the trees ..." he whispered, running his fingers over the painting. Dishonest *rapins* could have taken advantage of his infirmity to give him smears: not one did. This old man with dead eyes commanded respect.

Despite everything, Father Angély did not get rich. Two or three years after the Great War, he died miserably before his collection rose in value. His Utrillos, his Modiglianis, his Dumonts have been dispersed (or perhaps they should have been rolled into his coffin?); he himself disappeared in a mass grave in Saint-Ouen or elsewhere, and his name, little by little, slipped into oblivion. However, over the years, his enigmatic silhouette still intrigues me.

And then we arrive at this beautiful passage:

What was he waiting for, on the bank of the rue Lepic, "watching" the wind for hours? Perhaps he was playing a role we never suspected. An augur? A soul weigher? A mysterious playmaker? ... His very presence forced us to think. Like him, we were looking for our way; we were struggling in the dark. And he taught us that true light is only found in itself ...

What does it matter! Maniac or phantom, he remains attached to the history of bohemia, and I push him into the circle of painters he has loved. So everything becomes clear at the end, as in an apologue: young and old, the inspired and the doers, the unlucky and lucky, the future masters and the failures, led to their destiny by a blind man crazy for colors.[8]

In *La Vie Passionnée de Modigliani* (1957), the French poet and art critic André Salmon (1881-1969) describes a scene in which both Modi and Dorgelès are drinking with a small group inside the Lapin Agile. Although Modigliani doesn't mention Angély by name, he describes the collector as an "old man" who "still buys, though he complains that he isn't able to enjoy his collection as much as he used to because his eyes are giving out. What happens to people's eyes when they can't see anymore? Who knows but that this old fellow doesn't see far more beautiful things than the canvases he buys?"[9] Salmon was well-acquainted with Modigliani, but since this chronicle contains long imaginary dialogues as well as colorful interior monologues, it's impossible to know for certain whether the conversation actually took place or was the result of poetic license.

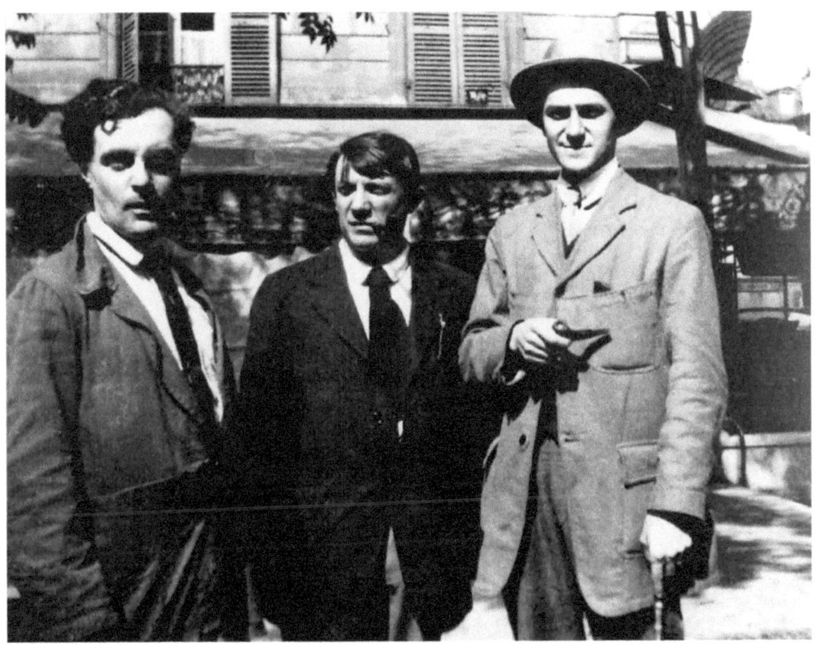

From left to right: Modigliani, Picasso, and André Salmon standing in front of the Café de la Rotonde, Paris, 1916. Photo by Jean Cocteau.

In 1960, Jean-Paul Crespelle (1910—1994), a journalist who created vivid accounts of the Belle Époque artists of Montmartre and Montparnasse, published *Modigliani: Les femmes, les amis, l'œuvre*. With a nod to Dorgeles' "Le destin est-il aveugle?," the title of Crespelle's fourth chapter, "Un Amateur Aveugle" (A Blind Amateur), is an homage to Angély:

> I only have one fan, and he's blind! ... Modigliani said with bitter humor.
> Which was both true and false. It was true that a collector bought paintings and drawings from him. Léon Angély, called "Father Léon," was a little old white-haired man whose figure was familiar to the people of the Butte. A

retired clerk, he lived in a tiny apartment on rue Gabrielle filled with bric-a-brac. He was a kind of passionate second-hand "Cousin Pons," who spent most of his retirement buying paintings from the artists he met in the bistros around Place du Tertre. His taste was surprisingly good, but he never offered more than ten francs for a painting.

This passion was not a disinterested one. Father Léon, not without reason, had told himself that among the *rapins* of Montmartre there would be some who would achieve success. So one day he might find himself commanding a collection that would be worth a fortune. His plan might have worked if he hadn't lost his sight and, little by little, had gone blind. Despite this handicap, he refused to give in to bad luck and continued to buy paintings.

Leaning on the shoulder of a young girl who served as his guide, he went to the studios and had the paintings described to him. From what the little one told him, he made his choice, relying on his flair. It is remarkable that the *rapins* presented him only with works of quality; they made it a point of honor not to give him mere daubs.

In the end Father Léon was punished for his venal love of art. As the war depleted his resources, he was forced to sell his Modiglianis and Utrillos. He had nothing left when he died: it was in 1921, just when the popularity of the artists he had discovered began to soar. A few more years and Father Léon would have died a millionaire![10]

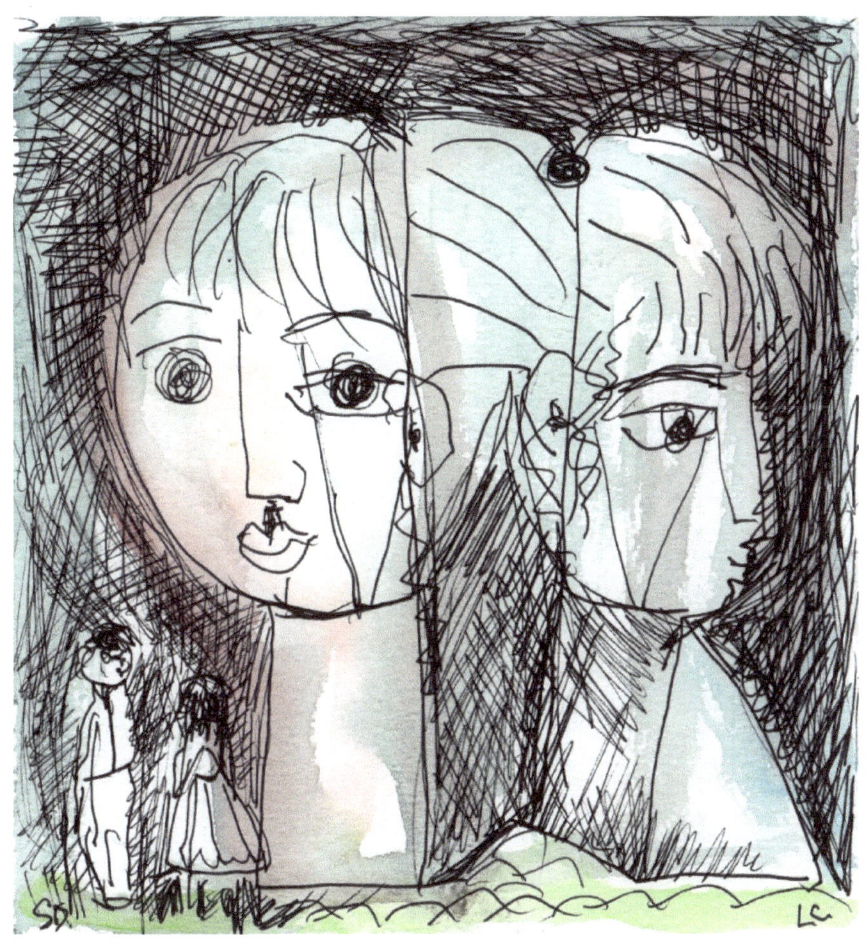

Sylvette David. *Father Angély et la fillette à côté du Buste de Sylvette in Greenwich Village*. Devon, England. December 2021. Watercolor and India ink on Langton watercolor paper, 8 ¼ x 7 ½ inches.

The mention of "rapins" (artist apprentices) offering works of quality echoes the words of Dorgelès. And the thematic structure of this entry, as well as Crespelle's reference to "Cousin Pons," makes it clear that he's relying on the urtext of Modigliani biography, *Artist Quarter* (which he includes in his bibliography, along with Dorgelès' *Bouquet de Bohème*). But he adds a tantalizing new ingredient: *une fillette* (a little girl).

Crespelle features this same account (with a few alterations) in his 1978 publication, *La Vie Quotidienne à Montmartre au Temps de Picasso: 1900–1910*. There he adds that Angély was an "assiduous visitor to the workshops of the Butte. A neighbor of Max Jacob, he lived in a tiny workshop on rue Gabrielle cluttered with ragpicker's junk."[11]

Max had moved from the Bateau Lavoir to rue Gabrielle in 1912. Therefore, it's unlikely that he would have provided the original introduction between Angély and Picasso while he was Léon's neighbor, since Angély would have been buying Picassos only during the earlier years, when the artist was offering his work at lower prices.

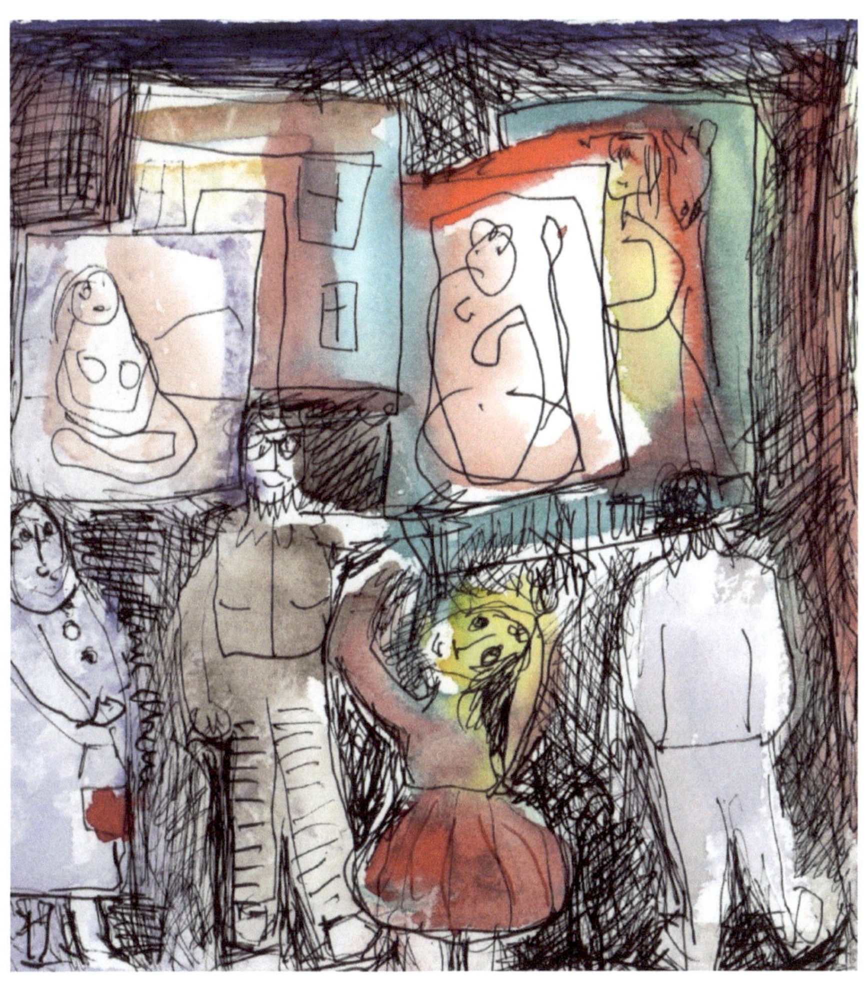

Sylvette David. *Le Père Angély and Joséphine*. **Devon, England. December 2021. Watercolor and India ink on Langton watercolor paper, 8 ¼ x 7 ¼.**

*　*　*

Four years after the appearance of Crespelle's *Modigliani,* a Polish writer named Thaddeus Wittlin (1909—1998) published a "biographical novel": *Modigliani: Prince of Montparnasse* (1964). A courageous man, Wittlin joined the Polish army in 1939 but was captured by the Russians and imprisoned in Soviet camps. After the war he briefly worked for Radiodiffusion Française, a Parisian radio station, then expatriated to America. During the Cold War he composed dramatic scripts for the Voice of America and Radio Free Europe.

Wittlin's *Modigliani* features a passage about Angély and his mysterious young guide that runs four-and-a-half pages – a bountiful harvest as compared to the meager pickings in the publications that precede it. According to a blurb on the dust jacket, "Material for this novel … is based on letters, family papers, and interviews with the Modigliani family by the author." But since it's a *novel,* we have no way of knowing when the narration faithfully mirrors reality or when it's interwoven with fanciful, richly embroidered fiction. It's even penned in the third-person omniscient point of view, so the reader is privy to every thought and feeling that sweeps through its various characters.

Wittlin begins his account of Angély by placing Modigliani – portfolio in hand – on rue des Saints Pères, thus anticipating the appearance of the saintly "Père" Angély. But the reference to the street isn't merely plucked from the ether. In Jeanne Modigliani's 1958 biography of her father, she writes that in 1906 three of Modi's paintings were on exhibit in the Art Gallery, located near the corner of rue des Saints Pères and the Boulevard Saint Germain. The shop was run by Laura Wylda, an English poet.[12]

In Wittlin's narrative, at first the artist goes searching for Madame Wylda, having yet to make her acquaintance. Upon discovering that she's away and that her shop is boarded up, Modi – now overcome by hunger while nibbling on the remains of a bread roll – wonders where he might unload a few of his sketches in order to feed his aching belly.[13]

What follows is the most colorful portrait ever rendered of Léon, and the one from which we learn the name of the girl who accompanied him into that Belle Époque labyrinth packed with artistic treasure:

> "Where could I sell something? Wait ... Bucci[14] mentioned someone not long ago on whom he'd fobbed off a watercolor. Who was it? The same man who bought the first things done by Picasso, Braque, Gris, and Wasley. What was his name? Père ... Frédé? No. Père Frédé runs the Lapin Agile. Père Azon? No. He's the one with the eatery on the rue de Trois Frères. Hell! Everybody in this damn Paris is some kind of *père*. Oh ... ! Père Léon in the rue Gabrielle ... Off to the rue Gabrielle!"

The author describes the street as seen through the eyes of Modigliani, who espies a "narrow alley, as tiny as a littered courtyard." There he encounters children playing, who direct him to Léon. "In that house," they inform the artist, "at the very top." Jumping and skipping along with him, they escort the hopeful painter to the building.

Modi climbs to the top floor and knocks on the single door at the landing. Judging by the way in which Wittlin paints the scene, one assumes that Léon's abode is a *chambre de bonne*: that classic Parisian garret that offers basic shelter to so many marginal, impoverished tenants (some achieving their first foothold in Paris; others tenaciously grasping their last). Wittlin describes it as a "gloomy," "murky attic": a grubby single room stuffed to the gills with assorted paraphernalia.

> At a kitchen table stood a young girl holding a pot over a spirit stove. She was ugly, uncombed, and clad in an unbuttoned dress. Angély scurried to the back of the room, which was cluttered with old furniture, frames, and pictures.
> "Do make yourself comfortable."

Modi settles on a windowsill and introduces himself as a "professional artist" whose work was recently exhibited at La Grande Chaumière (a celebrated artist's school, still in existence in Montparnasse). Attempting to enter into the collector's good graces, he adds: "My friends told me you're an art lover who discovered Matisse and Cézanne. Picasso speaks of you as a real expert." To which Léon replies:

> "But what kind of an expert am I? Simply a collector. I always loved to own pictures which pleased me. I spent practically all of my small earnings as a tax official on them. Once, I myself tried to paint. Every Sunday I would go to the Seine with my easel and palette. Joséphine, get moving and pour us a glass. You'll have a drink, won't you? I used to imagine that if I had a one-man show, the *Figaro* would carry an article entitled 'Modest Clerk – Great Artist.' But I had no talent. *Merci*." He took the glasses from the girl's hand, gazing at her with a fatherly expression. "But then I had to drop my one pleasure because my eyesight was failing. And that was the disability that befell me, a man who loves painting."

But Léon admits that he's driven as much by a love for art as he is by an ardent desire to gamble:

"Now, since I've retired, I use my pension to buy the works of young people, because you never know. It may happen that suddenly there will arise a new Ingres or Toulouse-Lautrec, or perhaps on a painted-over canvas I'll discover a Rembrandt or a Botticelli. I'll be able to sell it at a profit and go to Nice for the rest of my life. Obviously I'll take Joséphine. Dear girl."

"Your daughter?

"No, a friend." He raised his glass. "*Santé!* A daughter wouldn't stay with her father like this."

"*A la votre!*" Amedeo could barely hide his amazement.

Léon then asks to inspect Modi's work:

Père Angély put on wire-framed glasses and stuck the drawing under his nose. "Hm, must be very delicate lines, for I can scarcely make out anything." He pushed his glasses up on his forehead and put the sketch to his red eyelids. "No. Nothing doing. I told you I was almost blind. I can make out your features at this distance. But such fine drawing, no. Joséphine, come here. What's this?"

The girl drew near and looked over his shoulder. "A young woman, to the waist. In pencil."

"Good?"

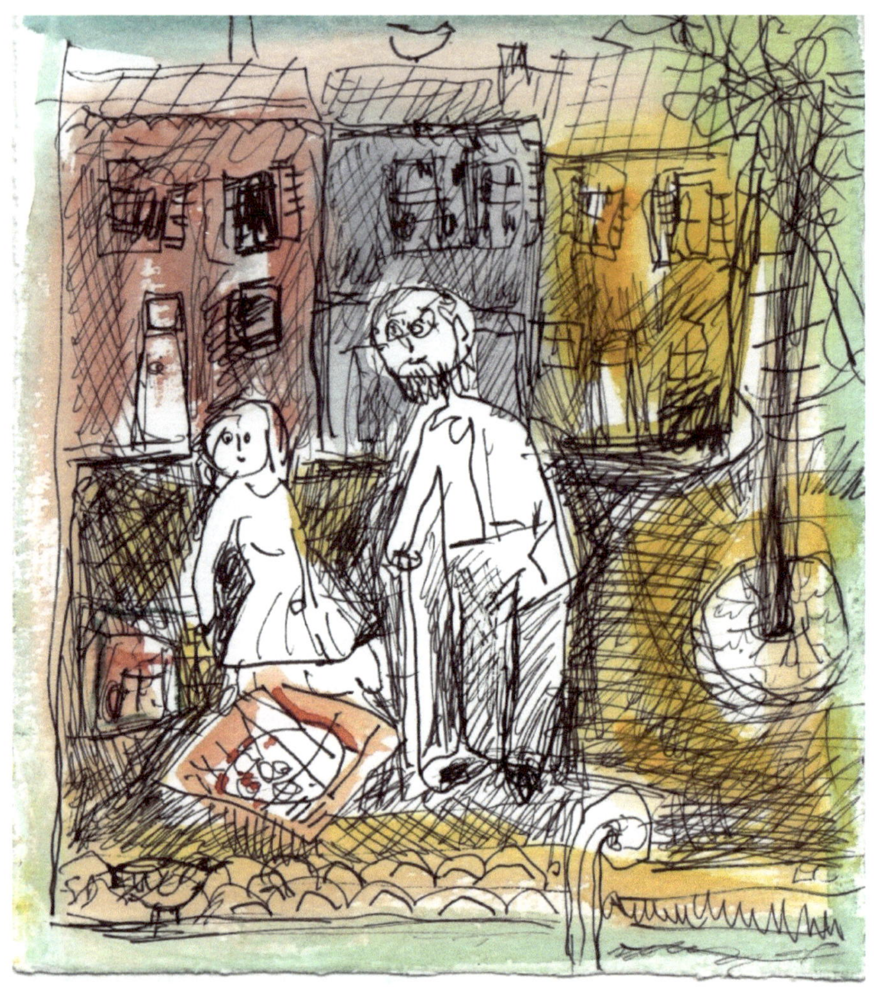

Sylvette David. *Le Père Angély and Joséphine Viewing Paintings at the Place du Tertre*. Devon, England. December 2021. Watercolor and India ink on Langton watercolor paper, 8 x 7 inches.

"Good." It never crossed her mind that she could dare to criticize the work of such an elegant gentleman. "A sad blonde with bare breasts."

"And the breasts, are they small or large?"

"Average." Joséphine shrugged. "Some might call them large."

"I'll buy it. What else do you have?"

"Here is a head of Anselmo Bucci, whom you know. Tempura."

"No, thanks. Anything else?"

"A standing nude."

"Joséphine, what do you say?"

"Long legs."

"I'll take it. What else?"

"A nude of Mado. The girl who used to pose for Picasso."

"What is it like, Joséphine?"

"She's lying stretched out with her hand on her belly."

"Is she covering herself?"

"Not completely."

"Good. Anything more?"

"This is a lady sitting on a bench, with a book," Amedeo explained.

"Young and pretty."

"In a hat, and no eyes, but yes," Joséphine volunteered.

"No eyes—then I don't want it. Something else?"

"Crouching nude," said Modigliani.

"Oh, that may not be bad. What do you think of it, Joséphine?"

"Not bad."

"All right. Next?"

Modigliani suddenly felt deeply humiliated by the judgments of this dull girl. He felt sorry for the drawings he had sold as dirty pictures designed to excite old men. He would have preferred to have them rejected as unappreciated works of art. "That's about all there is of interest." He shut his folder. "The rest are unfinished sketches."

While haggling over a price for the four drawings selected by Angély, Modi requests "fifteen francs a piece."

"What? That much?" The old man was sincerely frightened. There was no doubt that the sum far exceeded his means. "Sixty francs in all? That's a fortune! Don't you see the conditions I live in?"

After some additional quibbling, they settle on a sum of twenty francs: as Modigliani glumly notes, "only five francs per drawing." But hunger has gotten the better of him, and Léon's crafty refusal to budge has paid off. How well Léon must have known that an artist's penury is a dealer's best friend!

The old man raised the straw mattress near the pillow and pulled out an old vest in which he kept his cloth wallet. From among receipts, prescriptions, letters, and documents he picked out a folded banknote. He straightened it out, and peered at it through his glasses. Still he wasn't completely sure. "Joséphine, is this definitely twenty francs?"

"Definitely."

"Please." He handed Modigliani the money.

"*Merci*, Monsieur Léon." Amedeo rose to leave.

"Give my regards to Picasso and tell him to drop in to see me."

"Very well. I shall."

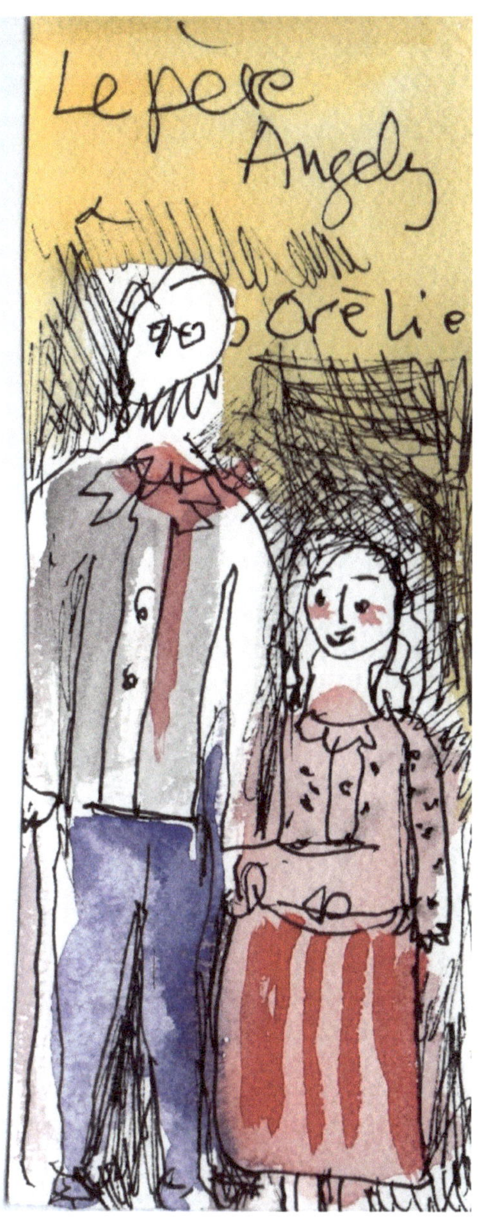

Sylvette David. *Le Père Angély and Joséphine (II)*. **Devon, England. December 2021. Watercolor and India ink on Langton watercolor paper, 8 x 3 inches.**

How fitting that Joséphine also serves as a guide to inspect Léon's bills of currency! Note the double-barreled irony when she describes a portrait as having "no eyes" (referring to Modigliani's signature style of rendering eyes without pupils) and of Léon, so dependent on another's perception, retorting: "No eyes – then I don't want it"![15]

A dozen years later, le Père Angély makes a brief appearance in William Fifield's (1916—1987) hefty biography, *Modigliani* (1976). An author of literary novels, short stories, and essays, Fifield conducted *Paris Review* interviews with Picasso, Jean Cocteau, and Robert Graves. (A Chicago native who was briefly married to the actress Mercedes McCambridge, [16] he was also regarded as a "one-time passable bullfighter.")[17] Fifield's book on Modigliani is based on conversations with Braque and Diego Rivera; with Modigliani's family; and with the artist's most important model, Lunia Czechowska. Publicized as a "definitive" biography, it was widely reviewed and hailed by the *New Yorker* as the "most accurate account … of one of our modern giants."

Just before introducing the reader to Angély, Fifield happens to mention the fact that Picasso's friend from Barcelona, Isidro Nonell, had lived on rue Gabrielle. (We shall return to this in a moment.) Then we meet Angély, who, despite having "nearly gone blind,"

> went on buying young painters, without much judging, for they were very cheap, and certainly he would one way or the other get a winner. He did own paintings that would one day have been worth an immense fortune, but he had to sell, including the Modigliani, during the First World War, and died a pauper.[18]

Once again, Angély's rudimentary biography is merely recycled from previous accounts, but the author's passing reference to Nonell remains intriguing. Although Fifield doesn't connect the dots, one wonders: Could Nonell's quotidian proximity to Angély (who also lived on rue Gabrielle) have led to Picasso's introduction to the collector? Nonell (who was eight years older than Picasso) died in 1911, so any introduction would have had to occur before then. And those were the years during which Picasso was often scraping by and searching for collectors. (But always with a bitter reluctance, because the French dealers so often short-changed him.) What makes it even more intriguing is that "Picasso stayed with Nonell at 49, rue Gabrielle"[19] during his first trip to Paris in 1900. Fifield was unaware of the fact that this is the same small building that housed le Père Angély.

The story of the visionary speculator and his equally gifted guide would later be revived in the widely celebrated scholarly works of John Richardson, a friend of Picasso whose companion, Douglas Cooper, had amassed the world's largest private collection of Cubism.[20] Richardson's decades-long association with the artist afforded him a unique perspective. Instead of the wooly-eyed pontifications that all too often make the discipline of art "history" a rather dubious venture, Richardson's writing is packed with insights that are directly rooted to this vital personal connection.

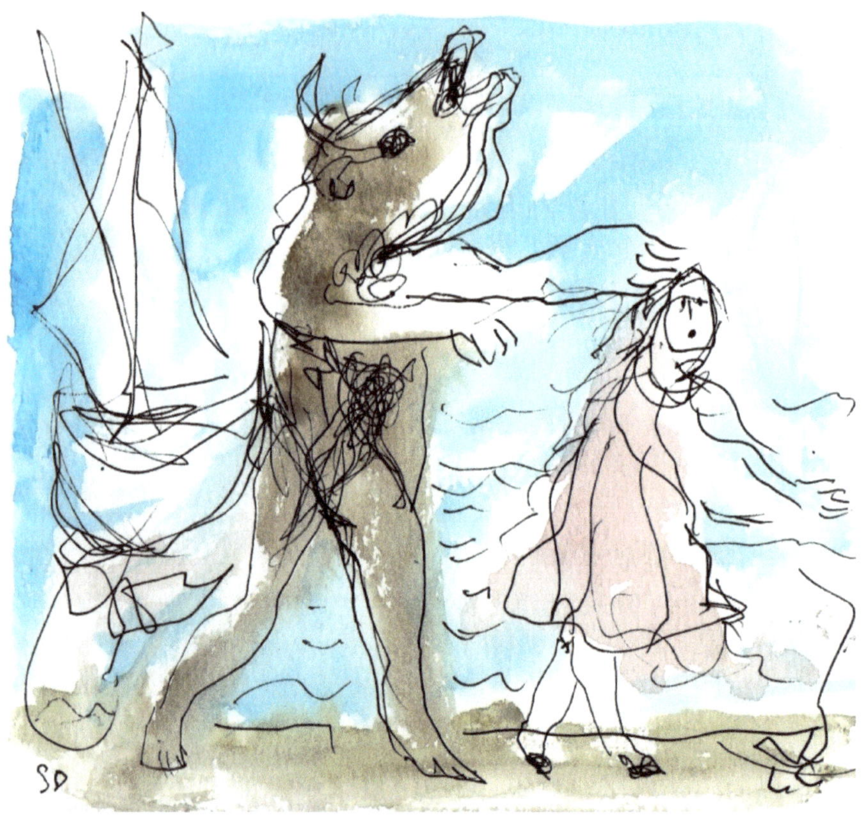

Sylvette David. *Blind Minotaur Being Led by a Little Girl (I)*. Devon, England. 3-6 February 2022. Watercolor and India ink on Langton watercolor paper, 8 x 8 ¼ inches.

In the first volume of his magisterial quartet, *A Life of Picasso* (1991), Richardson borrows directly from Crespelle's earlier account. While citing the work of his predecessor, he quotes Crespelle's phrase "stupendous flair" in referring to Léon's shrewd, uncanny ability. (Crespelle renders it as *"se fiant a son flair."*)

Richardson regards Angély as "not so much a dealer as a *dénicheur*: a talent scout or "spotter," and adds

> Picasso was fascinated by Angély: he was blind. A retired legal clerk of limited means, he spent his days going from one Montmartre atelier to another, led around by a little girl, who would describe the works he was being "shown." His "stupendous flair" is hard to credit. Maybe it was the girl who had it. At all events Angély's inspired speculation went unrewarded. World War I inflation forced him to unload his Picassos, Modiglianis, Utrillos and much else before prices took off. By the time he died (1921), he had nothing left. The little that Fernande tells us about le Père Angély's visits to the Bateau Lavoir suggests that Picasso may have drawn on memories of the sightless art lover and his child guide when (1934) he depicted a blind Minotaur being led around by a little girl.[21]

Utilizing his own remarkable flair, here Richardson introduces a new element into the equation: The birth of a blind Minotaur. He dangles this single sentence, then waits until the appearance of his fourth and final Picasso volume – thirty years later – to fully flesh it out. And note the sublime subtitle of this posthumously published masterpiece: *The Minotaur Years.*

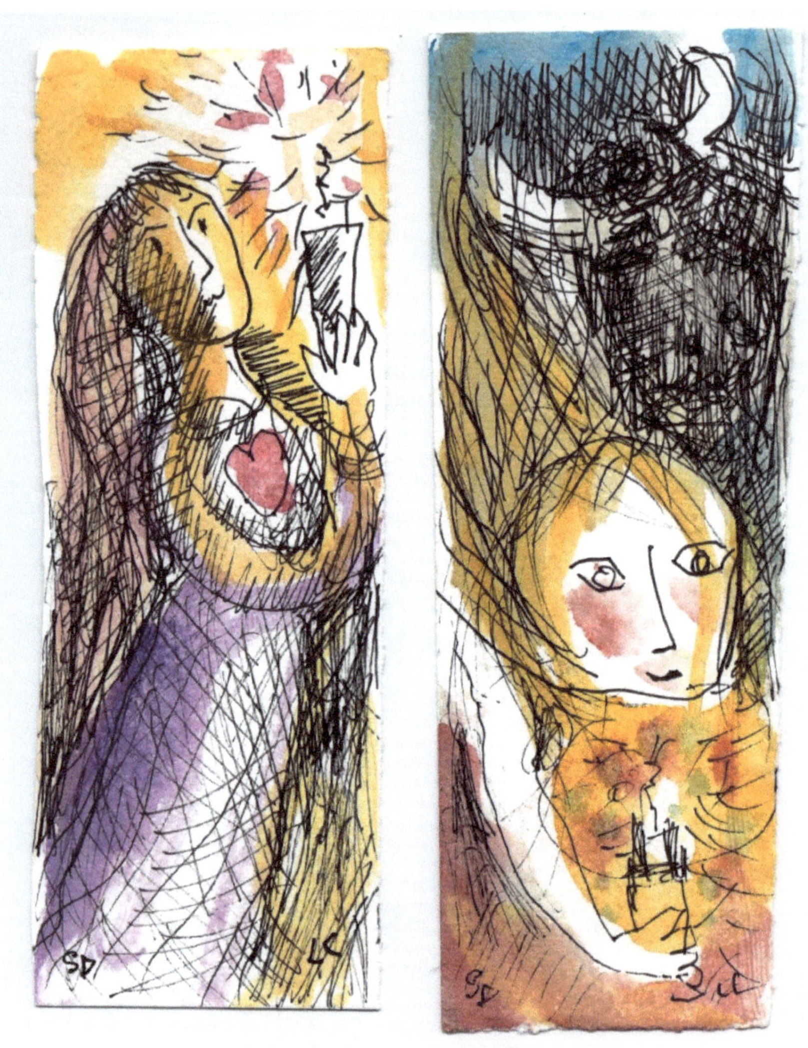

Sylvette David. Left: *Saint Lucy*. Devon, England. 4 December 2021. Watercolor and India ink on Langton watercolor paper, 7 ¾ x 2 ¾ inches. Right: *The Matador and the Light*. Devon, England. 4 December 2021. Watercolor and India ink on Langton watercolor paper, 8 x 3 inches.

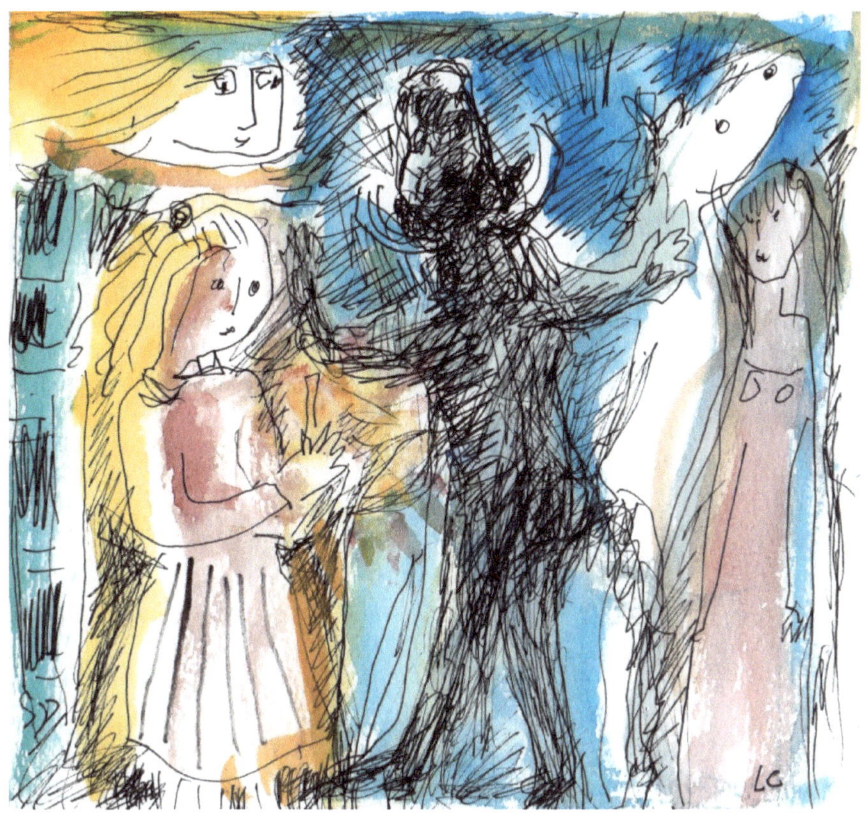

Sylvette David. *Blind Minotaur Being Led by a Little Girl (II).* **Devon, England. 3-6 February 2022. Watercolor and India ink on Langton watercolor paper, 8 x 8 ¼ inches.**

The Minotaur was also appropriated by artists and writers in the Surrealist movement. A minor figure in Greek myth, the "bull of Minos" was spawned by Pasiphaë, wife of King Minos, after being impregnated by a snow-white bull.

As is often the case with Picasso's work, the Minotaur drawings and engravings contain multiple layers of meaning, reference, and association. While the girl in this prototypical 1934 drawing may have been inspired by Angély's guide, Joséphine, her physical features are modeled on Picasso's athletic mistress, Marie-Thérèse Walter, whose likeness here is unmistakable. (Marie-Thérèse would become pregnant with Picasso's daughter Maya the following year.)

Richardson also informs us of another substrate of meaning: one lurking in the myth of Saint Lucy, "patron saint of the blind, whom many Spaniards held in superstitious awe." *Lucy* is the feminine form of *Lucius*, which is derived from the Latin, *lux*, or "light.")

> This early fourth-century martyr, who was in fact Sicilian rather than Spanish, had her eyes gouged out during the Roman Empire's final wave of Christian persecution. By the thirteenth century Saint Lucy had become a cult figure throughout Europe. Hence, echoes of her legend in *Blind Minotaur* and *Minotauromachie*. One of Picasso's erudite poet friends might well have told him about the role – small but significant – that Saint Lucy plays in Dante's *Divine Comedy*, when Dante begins to ascend the mountain of Purgatory, which emerges from a lake. On the lake's surface he sees a radiant boat floating on angels' wings carrying the souls of the redeemed. Dante soon falls asleep and upon waking is told by his guide, Virgil, that Saint Lucy has brought them to the gates of Purgatory.[22]

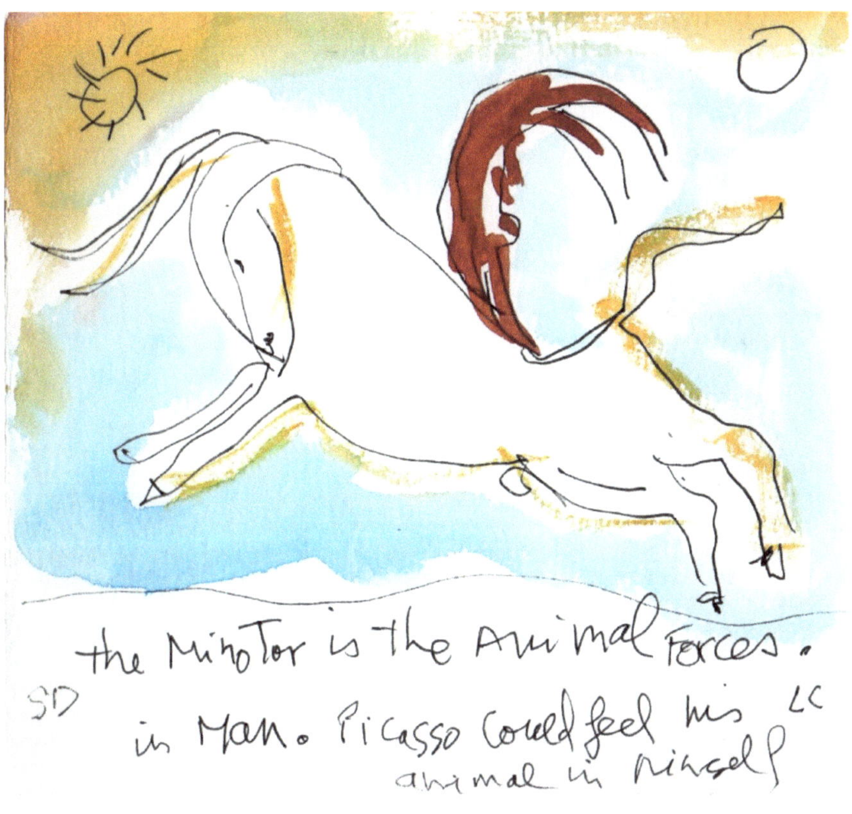

Sylvette David. *Twirling over the Bull*. Devon, England. 3-6 February 2022. Watercolor and India ink on Langton watercolor paper, 8 x 8 ¼ inches.

Besides Picasso's "erudite poet friends" there was also Modigliani, who was constantly quoting from Dante.[23]

Picasso's drawing of the blind Minotaur (reproduced in Richardson's final volume)[24] features three additional figures: a pair of boatmen docking a small vessel, and a girl leading a disembarked Minotaur from left to right along a shore. (Presumably, the Mediterranean.) While the sailors and beast are rendered with a handful of carefully chosen lines, the girl is portrayed in profile with far more abundant detail. (This profile view also allowed Picasso to fully exploit the sensuous contours of Marie-Thérèse's prominent nose: a signature shape in most of her portraits.) The broad expanse of bright, cloudless sky stands in contrast to a finely etched bouquet of flowers, grasped in the girl's right hand, and to the shadowy curves of her flowing, billowing dress.

A colossal Minotaur – whose frame fills the entire width of the page – trails behind. Its bulky girth and heavily outlined silhouette create another bold contrast to the emptiness of the surrounding landscape. Its right hand, gripping a walking stick, is clasped by the girl's tiny fingers, which she extends behind her back. The Minotaur's left hand rests upon her head, its gargantuan fingers cradling her silky hair.

Bearing a grave expression, the beast is portrayed with its head twisted to the side, tilted up at a forty-five degree angle. (The ever-observant Picasso must have known that this "head tilt" is a common symptom exhibited in certain forms of vision impairment.) The exaggerated dimensions of its oversized arms and hands highlight their importance, for now they function as tactile eyes: prehensile tentacles that reach toward the diminutive girl in a gesture of ultimate trust and dependence. One cannot help but wonder if le Père Angély felt something similar while standing beside his faithful *jeune fille*.

Although Richardson focuses on this particular drawing of the blind Minotaur, the series of engravings that compose Picasso's *Vollard Suite* feature many other versions of this exquisitely rendered monster, half man and half bull. According to Richardson, this amalgamated hybrid is also a stand in for the artist himself: an alter ego, among many others in his oeuvre. The "Minotaur" section of the Suite includes eleven etchings, while the "Blind Minotaur" section contains four, each expanding on the composition laid out in Picasso's preliminary sketch. In his Introduction to *Picasso's Vollard Suite*, Hans Bolliger describes three of the four "Blind Minotaur" engravings:

> an innocent little girl … is seen holding a bouquet (No. 94) and in another a dove, symbol of purity (No. 95). Silent spectators, benumbed by compassion, follow the scene. Most moving is the aquatint of the girl with the fluttering dove, leading the blinded Minotaur through the night (No. 97) – a work magnificent for its mood, its composition, its symbolic force, and its technical perfection. The fascination of this work is enhanced by the mysterious lights that seem to emanate from the bodies themselves.[25]

"If all the paths I have traveled along were marked on a map and joined with a line," Picasso once remarked, "it might represent a Minotaur."[26]

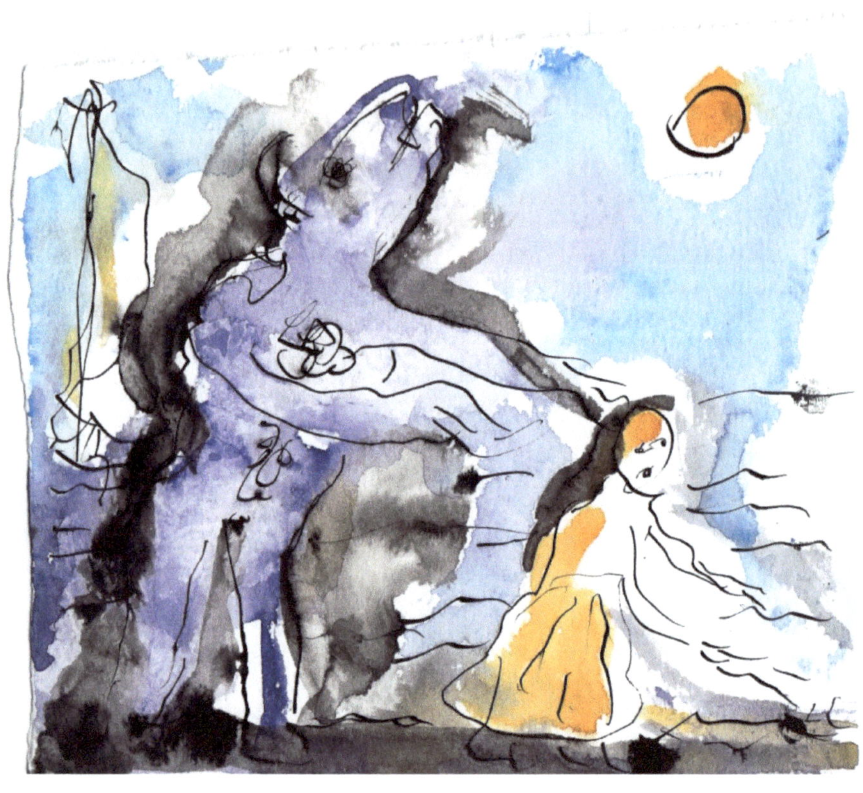

Sylvette David. ***Blind Minotaur Being Led by a Little Girl (III)***. Devon, England. 3-6 February 2022. Watercolor and India ink on Langton watercolor paper, 7 x 8 inches.

Although he died impoverished and nearly forgotten, le Père Angély helped to preserve what Richardson calls the "sacred stuff of art" – regardless of whether his motivation was merely pecuniary. Léon and Joséphine also inspired the greatest artist of the twentieth century. "The blind Minotaur," says Richardson, "would develop into one of his most moving and spectacular prints."[27]

Here the author refers to Picasso's 1935 engraving, *La Minotauromachie*.[28] The sixth state of the etching, it evolved through seven stages.[29] It features a bare-breasted Marie-Thérèse (then twenty-six years old, and pregnant with Maya) as a wounded *matadora* – spinning over the back of a bloodied horse as she "bares her chest and stomach to the Minotaur."[30] (According to Richardson, this may have been influenced by the ancient Cretan frescos of young athletes leaping over charging bulls with a carefully choreographed exactitude.)[31] This same composition also contains a second portrait of Marie-Thérèse, who appears at a windowsill, overlooking the scene, while seated beside her sister.

On the left side of the engraving another girl is depicted, facing the Minotaur. The main protagonist of the scene, in one hand she clutches a bouquet, reminiscent of the earlier images of Marie-Thérèse. In her right hand she upholds a burning candle or lantern. This powerful symbol – representing both the essential spark of consciousness that defines a human being and the inner light that guides us through our existential woes – is the focal point of the engraving.

The bold contrast of light and dark chiaroscuro – a highly developed skill that enlivens so much of Picasso's work – endows the bursting light with a "spiky" illumination.

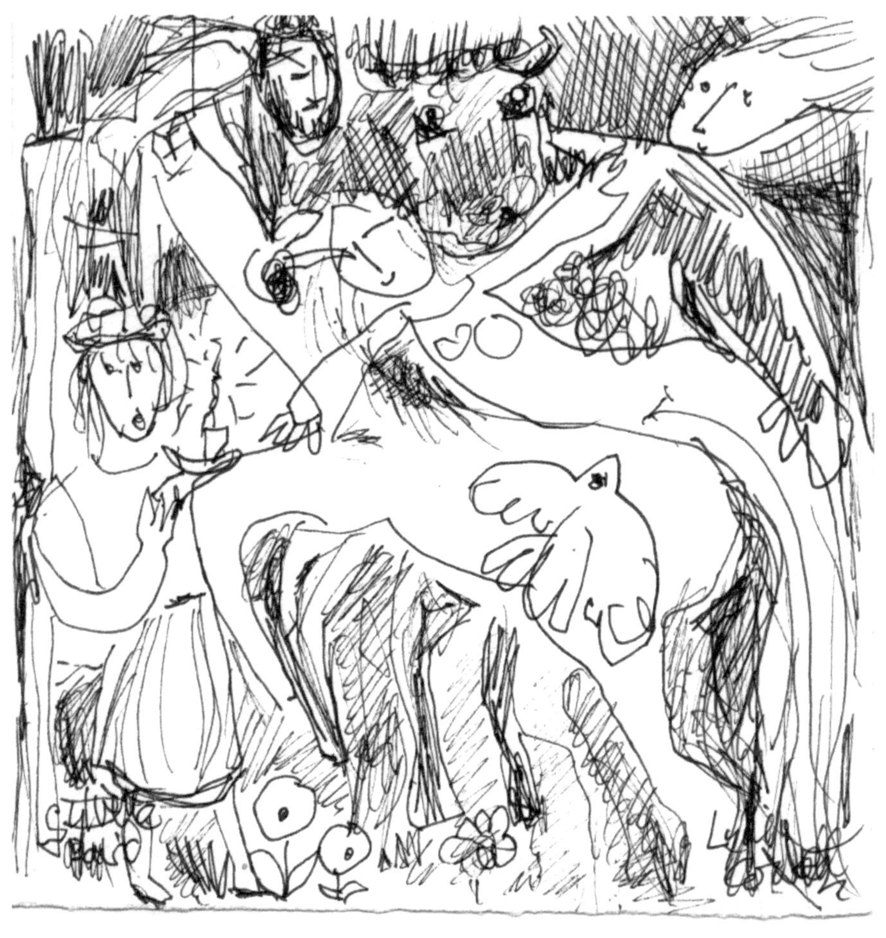

Sylvette David. *Thoughts with Lucy the Light*. Devon, England. December 2021. India ink on Langton watercolor paper, 7 ¾ x 7 ¼.

Richardson regards this as an iconic Mithraic motif: one that the artist applied wittingly, aware as he was of the power of myth and its underlying presence in art. In Mithraic legend, after a sacrificial slaying of bulls, the sun god's rays descend on Mithras, who then partakes in a banquet – consuming the hide of a bull – with this solar divinity.[32]

But the girl gripping the candle – dressed in attire that more resembles Spanish rather than French habiliments – isn't

Marie-Thérèse. Richardson identifies her as Conchita, Picasso's seven-year-old sister who died of diphtheria in 1895. While praying for her recovery, the fourteen-year-old Picasso made a vow: If God would spare her, he'd give up painting. But the artist broke his promise before she could recover; then she perished. Haunted by this broken vow and traumatized by her loss, it's not surprising that Picasso portrays Conchita throughout his oeuvre. But she's never been more movingly rendered than here, where

> her presence is central to the meaning of the composition. Conchita illuminates *Minotauromachie.* The Minotaur stretches out his right hand to grasp her light, but he fails to reach it. The flame represents the art Picasso had vowed to abandon if Conchita lived. In *Minotauromachie* he is unable to grab the emblem of his votive obsession. His broken vow would never be fully redeemed.[33]

Fortunately so – for what if Picasso had abandoned his calling? Our century of miracles would have been deprived of its most central illumination.

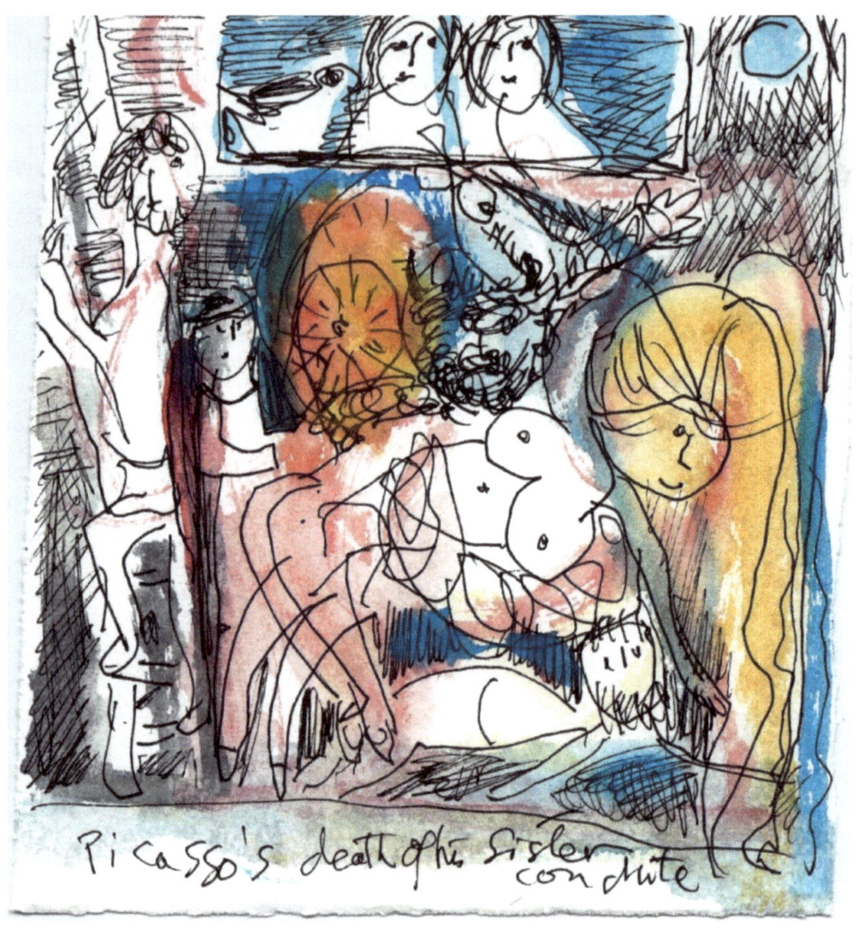

Sylvette David. *The Death of Picasso's Sister Conchita*. Devon, England. 1 December 2021. Watercolor and India ink on Langton watercolor paper, 8 x 7 inches.

Thus, the Minotaur and its diminutive companion represent Angély and Joséphine as well as Picasso, Marie-Thérèse, and Conchita. If we transpose their identities, perhaps we can conclude that Picasso is offering us a hint about his transcendental agenda. Like Angély, he is an augur who is blind to what will arrive next upon his canvas, yet he knows how to tease out its presence. Likewise, it is only through the animate Muse, personified and particularized in both Marie-Thérèse and Conchita, that he may accomplish his task.

*　　*　　*

Just as my research on Angély was coming to a close, I decided to search through the Ancestry website with the hope of chancing upon Léon's footprints. Lo and behold, a 1921 death certificate for Léon Angély popped up in Paris. As I enlarged the document, the words "rue Gabrielle" were visible in the neat, elegant handwriting of a forgotten *fonctionnaire*. It was the evening of 13 December 2021. Suddenly it occurred to me that a full century had passed since Léon's demise.

I carefully began my translation:

"On 12 May 1921, at 5:30 a.m., it [i.e., his death] was determined at 2 rue Ambroise-Paré, Léon Angély, living at 49 rue Gabrielle, born on 16 November 1848, legal clerk. [*Clerc d'avoué*.] Son of Annette Angély, deceased. Unmarried. Drawn up on 13 May 1921, 12:00 p.m. by the declaration of Louis Lemigout, 36 years old, and of Maurice Petit, 28, employees at 2 rue Ambroise-Paré, who have read and signed with us: Charles Veil, adjutant at the town hall of the tenth *arrondissement* of Paris."

The various accounts that we've examined so far have noted that Angély worked as a legal clerk, resided on the tiny rue Gabrielle, and died in 1921. Thus, there can be little doubt that this is the certificate of "le Père" Angély, who perished six months before his seventy-third birthday.

Trente-huitième Feuillet

Le douze Mai mil neuf cent vingt un, cinq heures trente, est décédé rue Ambroise Paré 2, Léon Angély, domicilié rue Gabrielle 49, né à Paris le seize Novembre mil huit cent quarante huit, clerc d'avoué. Fils d'Annette Angély décédée. Célibataire. Dressé le treize Mai mil neuf cent vingt un, douze heures, sur la déclaration de Louis Lemigout trente six ans et de Maurice Petit vingt huit ans, employés rue Ambroise Paré, 2, qui, lecture faite, ont signé avec Nous: Charles Veil, adjoint au Maire du dixième arrondissement de Paris. Lemigout

Death certificate

The tenth *arrondissement* is host to four hospitals; the second largest is the Hôpital Lariboisière. Founded in 1854 after the second cholera epidemic, its southern flank runs along rue Ambroise-Paré. Its official address is 2, rue Ambroise-Paré, so we may surmise that Louis Lemigout and Maurice Petit were employed there and perhaps witnessed Léon's death in a hospital bed. The northern side of the building borders Boulevard de la Chapelle, which is the southern boundary of the adjacent eighteenth arrondisse-ment: the Butte Montmartre. Léon's residence at 49, rue Gabrielle was two miles north of the hospital. (This is the same institution where Modigliani's friend, Dr. Paul Alexandre, had served as an intern.)[34]

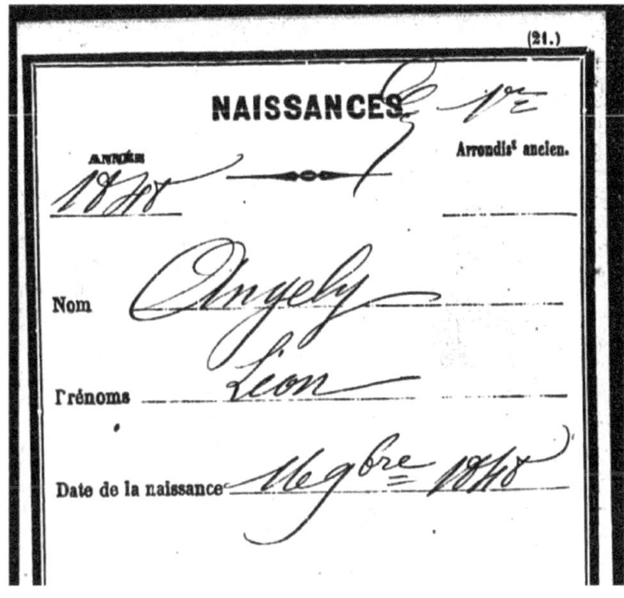

Birth record

With this information, I was able to uncover an additional civil record of Léon's birth (above).[35] Though it doesn't list his parents, it indicates that Léon was born in the first *arrondissement* on 16 November 1848: a month before the end of the 1848 Revolution, which led to the abdication of King Louis Philippe and the abolition of the French monarchy.

Picasso once remarked "In any age, there are only a handful who can truly see." Clearly, Père Angély was one of them.

Interment at Père Lachaise

A search in the online Paris Archives revealed that Léon was buried in Père Lachaise on 14 May 1921: the same cemetery where Modigliani was interred the year before.[36] Dorgelès' speculation that he was probably buried in a "mass grave, in Saint-Ouen or elsewhere," proved to be untrue, but his remark suggests that Léon's final resting place wasn't widely known.

Besides bearing Léon's name, the Père Lachaise gravestone is inscribed with the names of seven other relatives, including Anne Rigout (née Angély, b. 1828), and Louise Cheron (née Angély, b. 1832). Louise was Léon's maternal aunt; her sister Anne was Léon's mother, who was twenty years old when she gave birth to her son. Her name appears on Léon's death certificate as "Annette," but the document fails to mention anything about Léon's father. The absence of a father's name might suggest a so-called illegitimate birth, which could explain why Léon took his mother's maiden name.

Thanks to the information gleaned from this headstone, I was able to unearth the marriage certificate of Anne Angély and Léon Rigout. The union occurred on 28 January 1873, when Rigout was forty-seven years old and when Anne was forty-five: twenty-five years after the birth of her son. (Although it's a common French name, one wonders at the coincidence that her spouse was also named "Léon.")

According to the marriage certificate, Anne was the daughter of Gabriel Angély and Marie Claudine Peulot. Anne was born on 14 July 1828 in Toutry, Côte d'Or, Burgundy, France. She died in her Parisian domicile, located in the 11th *arrondissement* at 37, rue de Montreuil, on 8 December 1909.

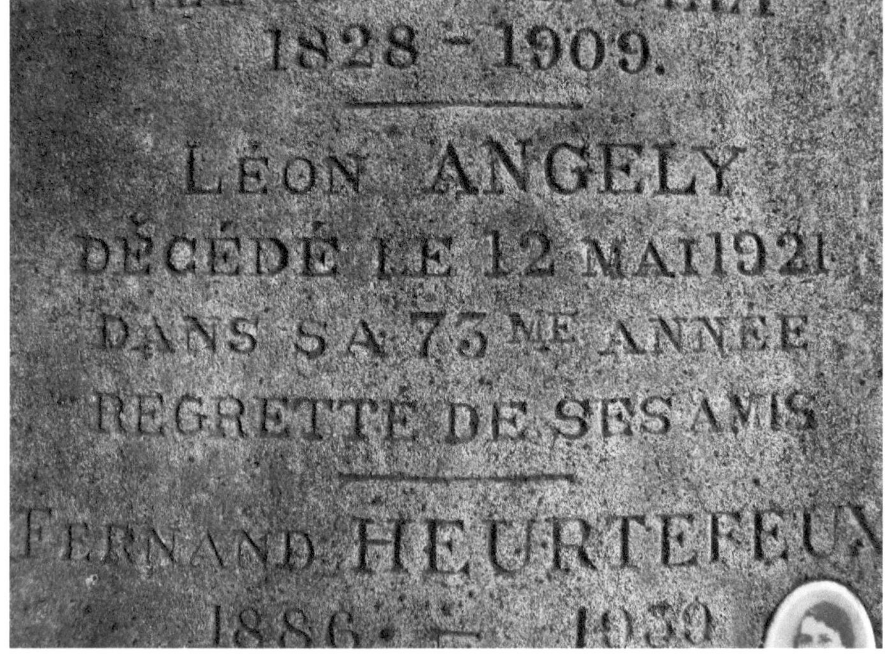

Photograph of Léon Angély's tomb, taken on 25 March 2022 by my colleague Céline Cardon, who tracked down the actual location of the grave. The epigraph "Regretté de ses amis" is fitting, as Léon, a childless *célibataire*, was survived by his friends in the art community. Besides Léon, his mother, and her sister Louise (Angély) Cheron, the other family members buried there appear to be Léon's in-laws from the Rigout and Cheron families. Photos Copyright © 2022 Céline Cardon.

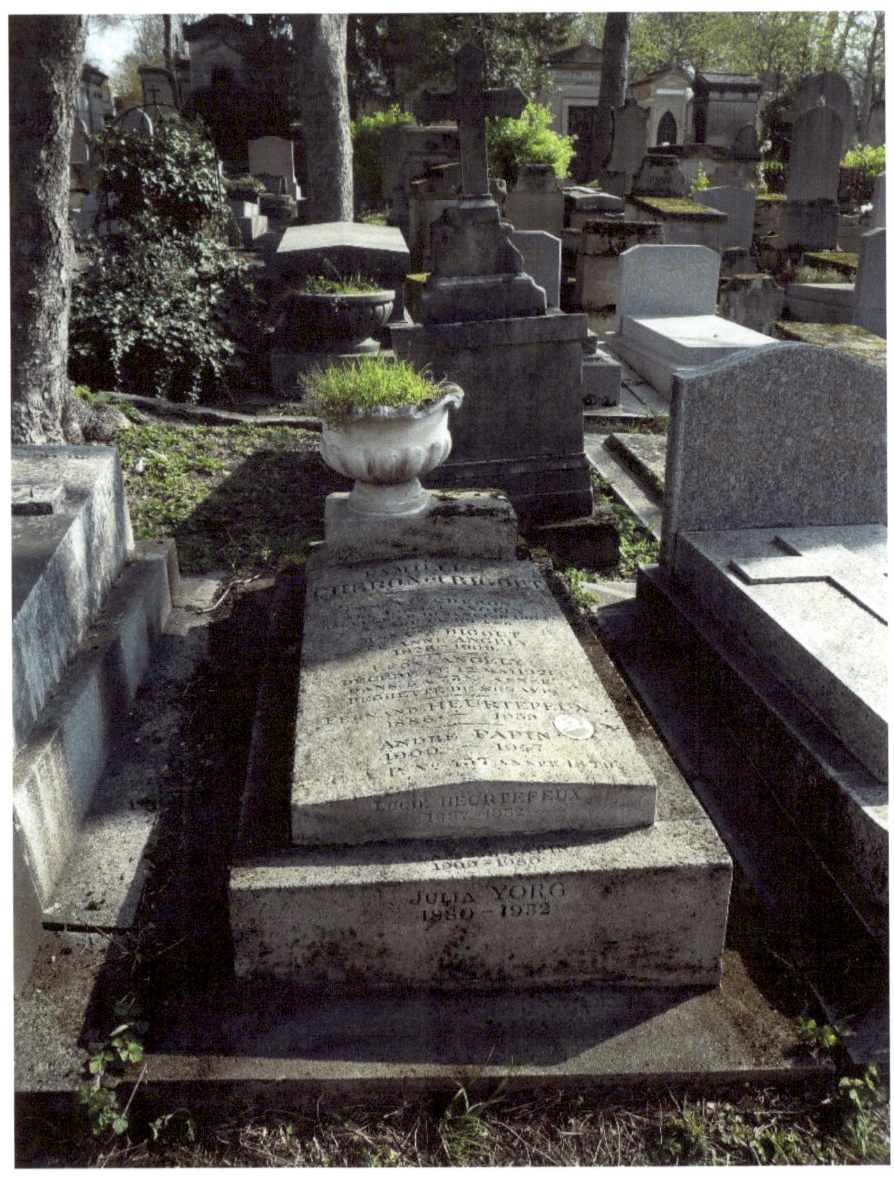

The last interment occurred in 1980. When Céline first arrived at the cemetery, the stone was encased in a bed of moss that completely obscured the engraving.

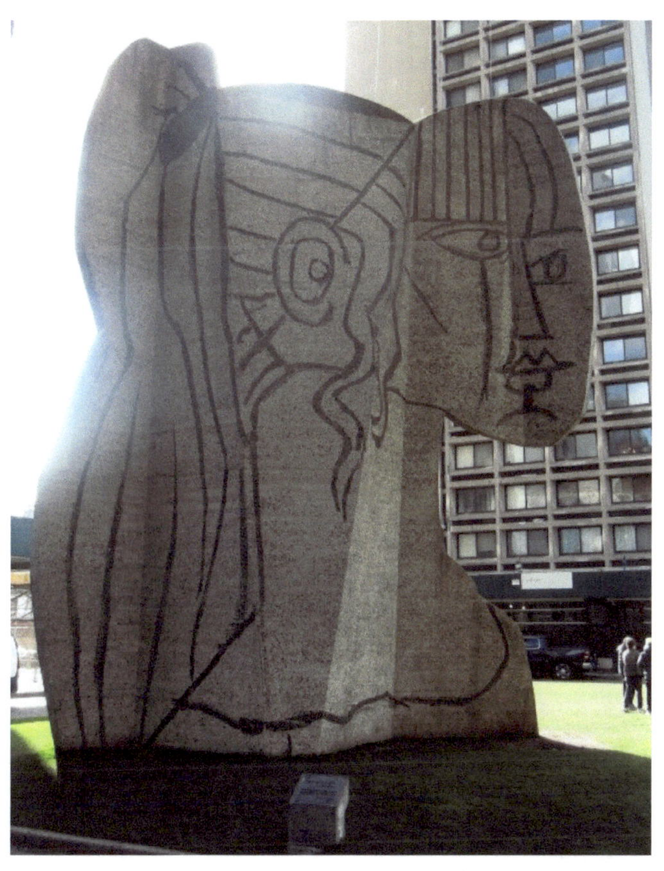

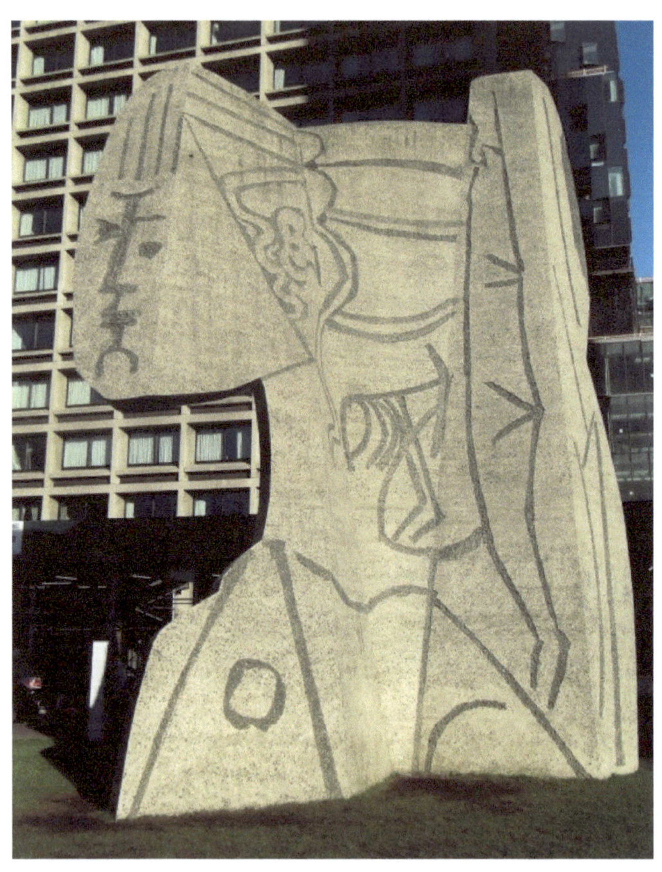

Sylvette David

I first became aware of Sylvette David thanks to "The Bust of Sylvette": a thirty-six-foot-high sculpture, commissioned by the architect I. M. Pei for the Silver Towers housing complex in Greenwich Village. (When Pei requested a piece by Picasso for the lawn, the artist responded by suggesting a "Sylvette.") Modeled after a two-foot-high sculpture that Picasso created from folded sheet metal in 1954, the "Bust" was constructed by the artist's official fabricator, the Norwegian sculptor Carl Nesjar, in 1968. [37] Weighing sixty tons, it's composed of concrete poured over black basalt pebbles. By sandblasting the cement surface and exposing the dark stones underneath, Nesjar re-created the effect of Picasso's line drawing of Sylvette that was embossed on the sheet metal *maquette*. Picasso was not only pleased by the result; he was also pleasantly surprised to learn of its durability. According to Nesjar's engineers, the construction is expected to last at least two thousand years.

Sylvette posed for Picasso in the spring of 1954 over a period of several months. The daughter of Emmanuel David, a Parisian art dealer, and Honor Gell, who was a painter, Sylvette was perhaps destined to have some sort of relationship with the art world. But her friendship with Picasso proved to be the great motivating force – arriving with the impact of a juggernaut – that inspired her lifelong devotion to painting.

As a native New Yorker, I often delighted in wandering through Manhattan's West Village; and, as I say, it was there that I first encountered the "Bust." After expatriating to Paris

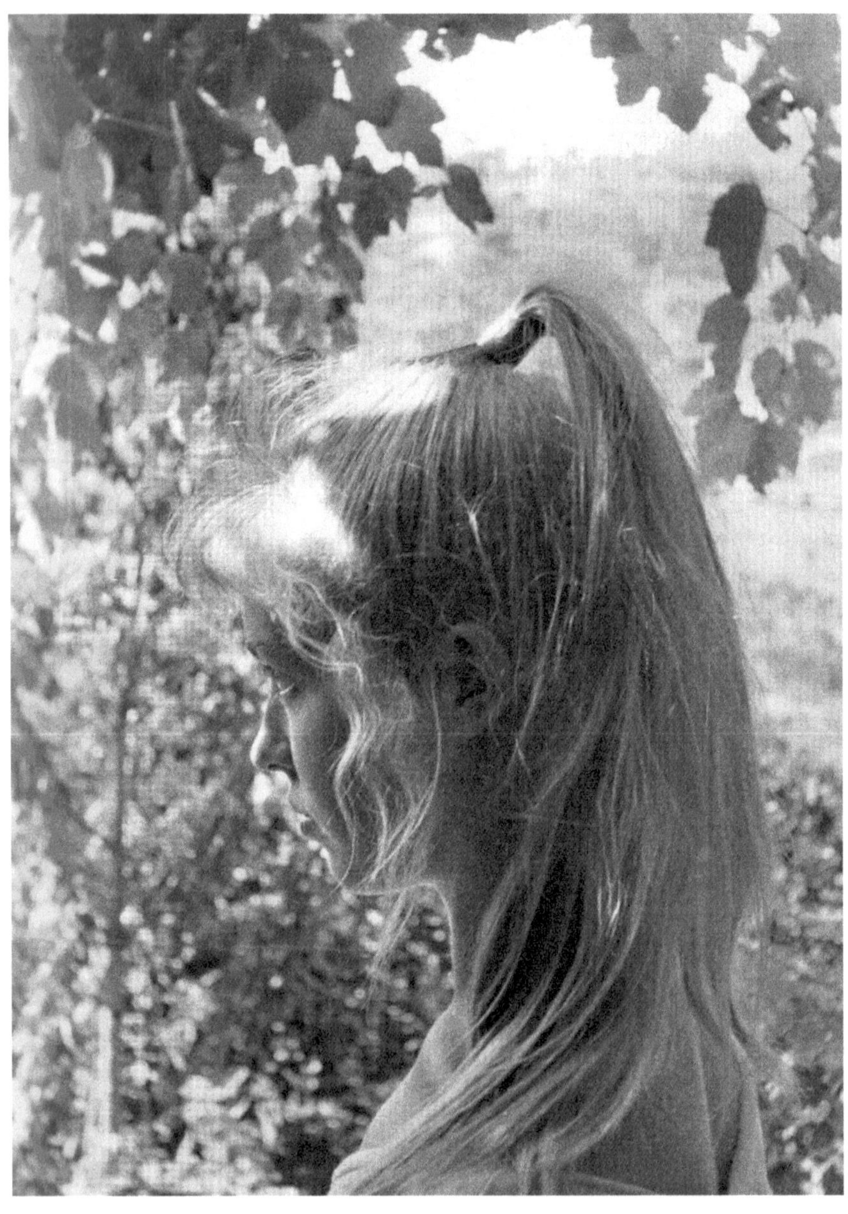

Sylvette David in Vallauris, France. Photo Copyright © 1954 Toby Jellinek.

at the end 1988 and paying numerous visits to the Musée Picasso in the Marais (a collection that includes a striking portrait of Sylvette from 1959, rendered in graphite pencil on vellum), the "Bust" soon came to serve an important function in my life. Over the next twelve years, whenever I'd return to New York for a brief visit, if I grew homesick for my beloved Paris I would ride the subway to Washington Square and then walk along Bleecker Street, where I'd enter lawn at Silver Towers. Seated on a low cement wall that runs perpendicular to the "Bust," I'd gaze with contentment. Some part of my lost Parisian world would be staring back at me through "Sylvette's" vast Cubist eyes, helping me to feel connected once again to Paris.

But how incongruous her presence seemed to be, positioned amidst the hustle and bustle of Manhattan! Skyscrapers loomed all around her; and, in the near distance, one could see the quaint wooden water towers lurking upon the rooftops of Soho. The "Bust" resembled an enormous puzzle that had washed up on the Manhattan shoreline after drifting from its moorings in the Mediterranean, like an ancient shipwreck marked with an indecipherable hieroglyph. And perhaps only Sylvette – the real, corporeal Sylvette, who was still alive and well – could help me to solve the puzzle. As I sat there daydreaming, I wondered if, one day, I might track her down and convince her to participate in an interview.

In 2014, the Kunsthalle Bremen museum hosted an exhibit titled *Picasso and the Model: Sylvette, Sylvette, Sylvette*, which featured over fifty Sylvette portraits. (Picasso had once informed the artist and writer Georges-Michel that there

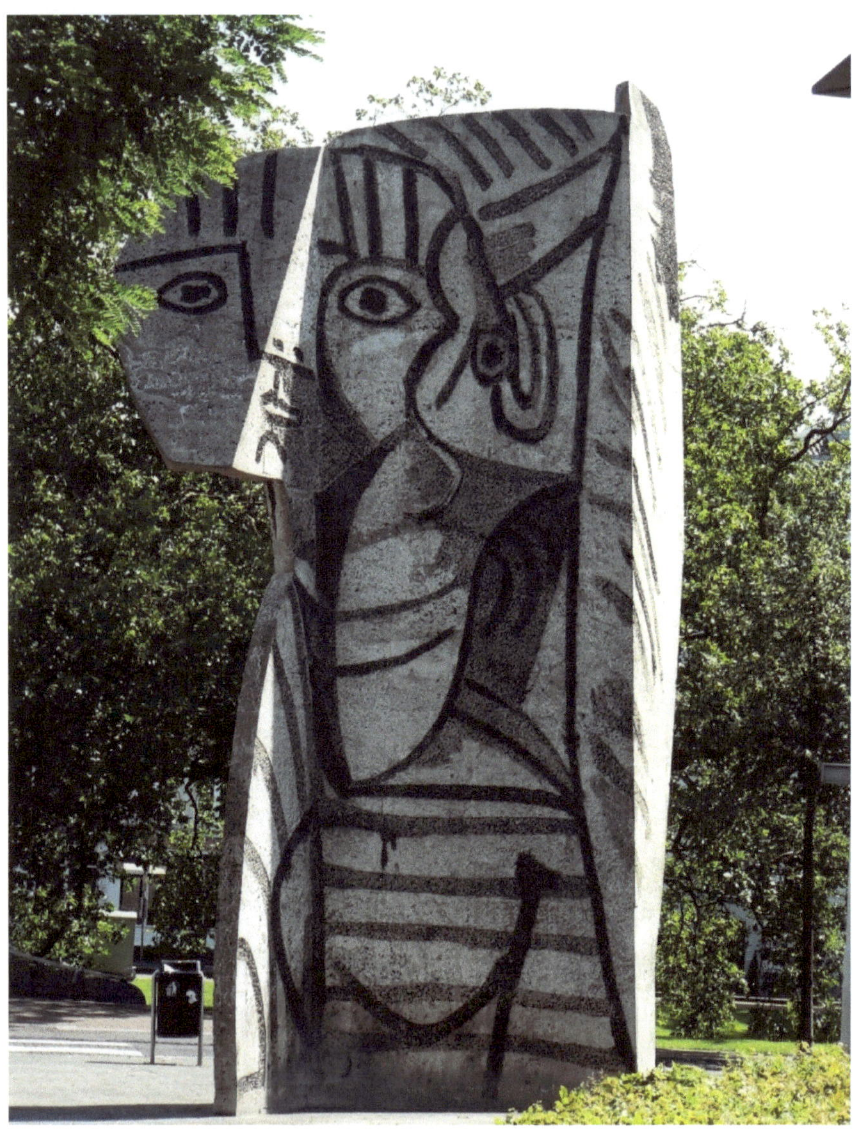

Picasso's *Sylvette* sculpture in Rotterdam. Fabricated by Carl Nesjar in 1970 from concrete and black basalt pebbles, it measures almost twenty-five-feet high.

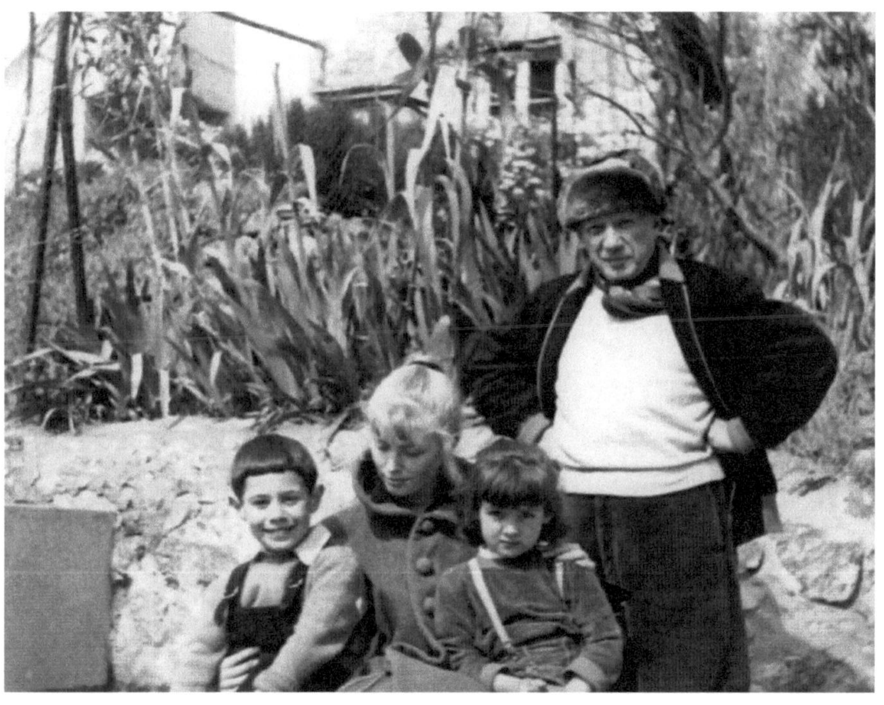

Sylvette, Picasso, and his children Claude and Paloma, at the villa La Galloise in Vallauris. Copyright © 1954 Toby Jellinek.

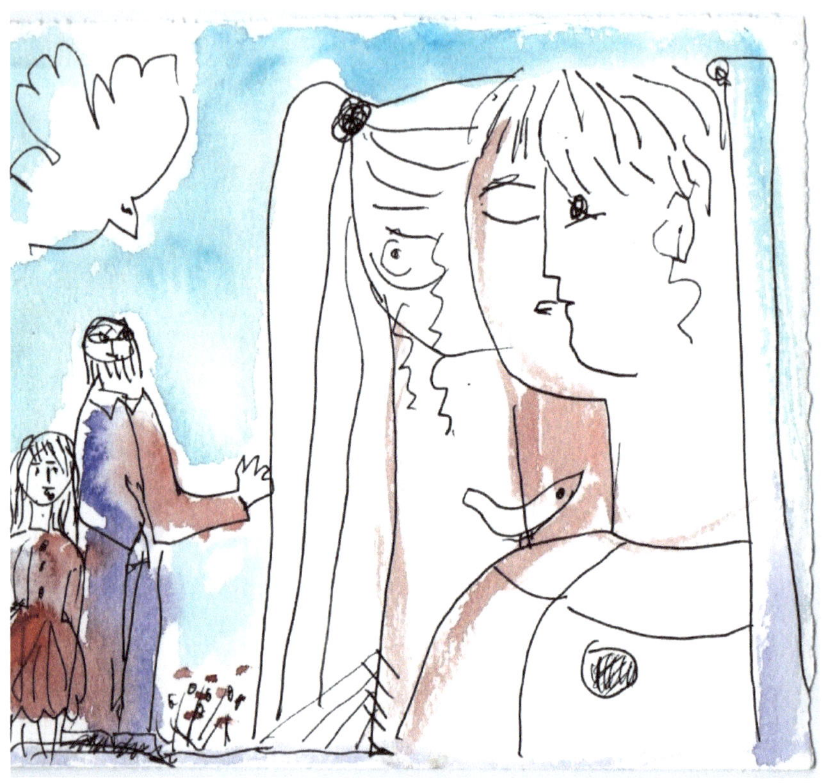

Sylvette David. *Sylvette in the Sky, with Père Angély and Joséphine*. Devon, England. December 2021. Watercolor and India ink on Langton watercolor paper, 7 ½ x 8 ¼ inches.

"Life goes on, and you die little by little. And you become like a cloud in the sky." – Sylvette David.

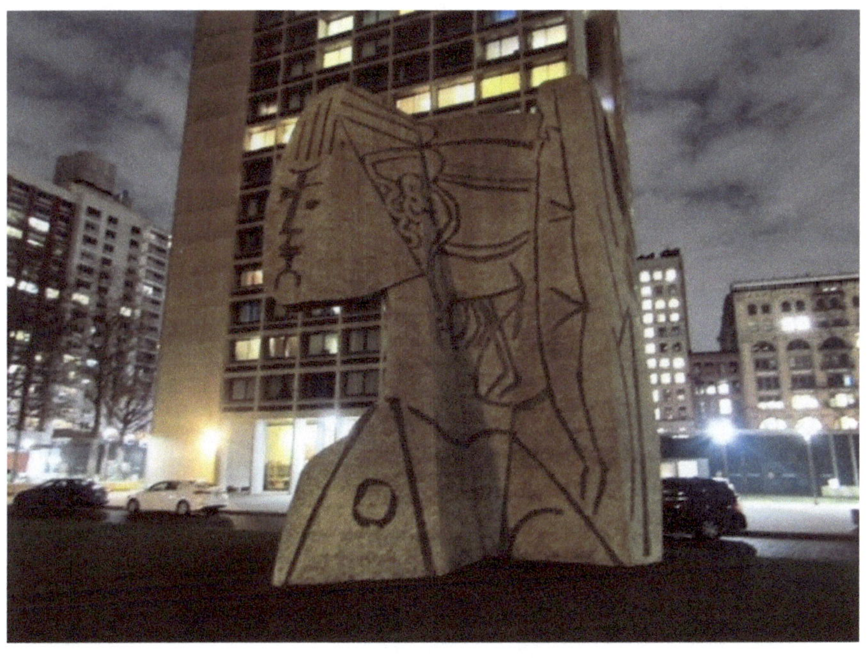

Picasso's *Sylvette* sculpture in Manhattan, constructed by Carl Nesjar in 1968. View facing east. Photo Copyright © 2017 Rob Couteau.

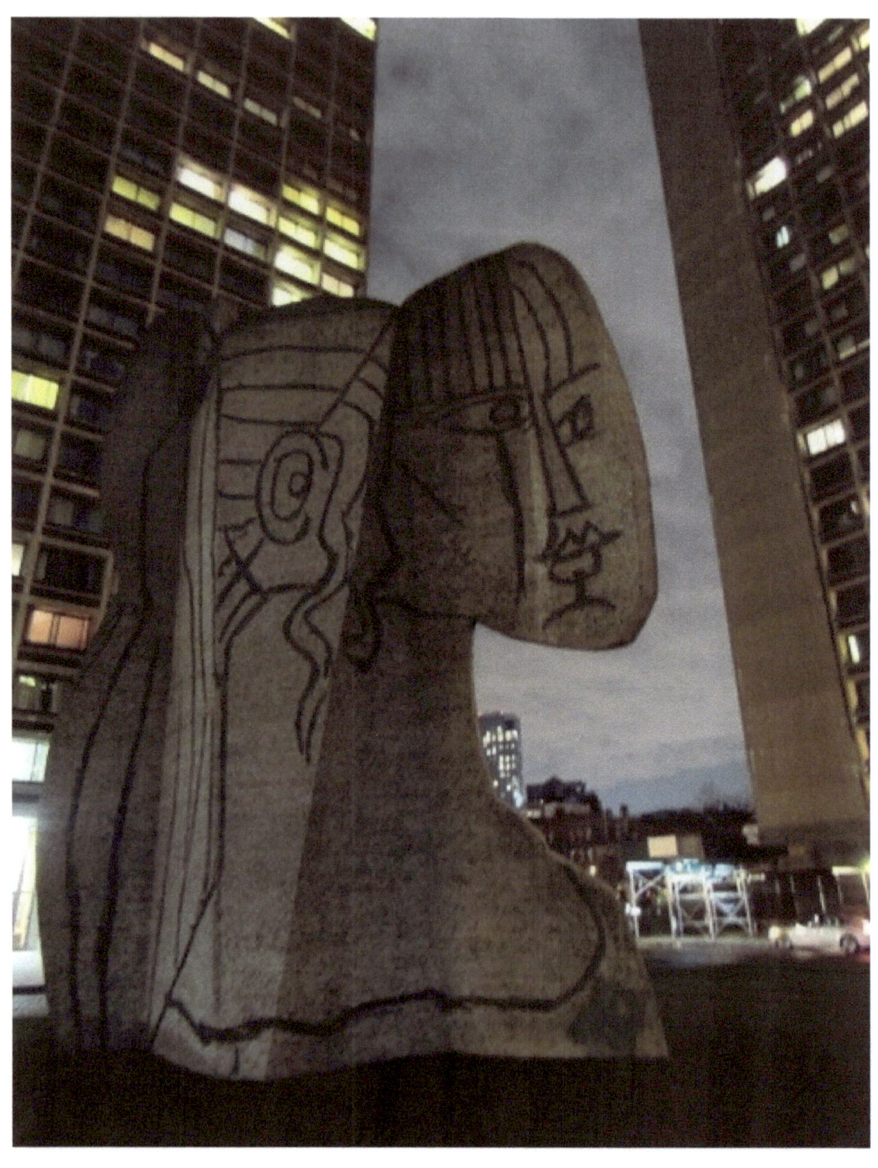

Picasso. *Bust of Sylvette*. **View facing west. Photo Copyright ©
2017 Rob Couteau.**

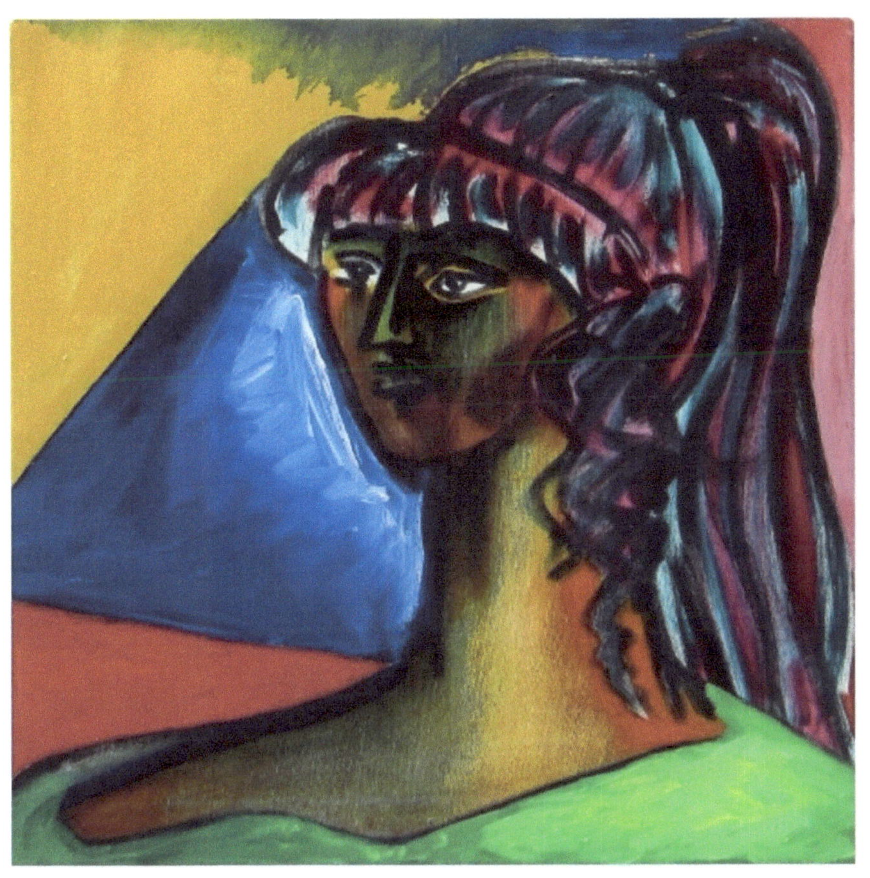

Rob Couteau. *Portrait of the Bust of Sylvette*. New Paltz, NY. 14 January – 3 August 2019. Oil on canvas. 20 x 20 inches. Collection of Sylvette David.

were "hundreds" of Sylvette sketches, but many have since been lost.) [38] Three years later, Sylvette's memoir, *I Was Sylvette*, was published in London, and I carefully devoured the text. The real Sylvette was now emerging and, for a number of reasons, I was deeply moved by her story.

That December I contacted Sylvette via her new website to request an interview. She immediately responded and suggested that I phone to schedule a talk. Though I hadn't prepared any questions, when I brought up the subject of the "Bust" she grew so excited that we immediately launched into a lengthy discussion.

"This is the first time that I've heard anyone talk about it!" she exclaimed. "Nobody seems to know there's such a big sculpture of me in New York; I can't believe it." The piece had always been of great importance to her, yet interviewers in the past had neglected to discuss it.

Thus began a dialogue that would continue over the years as our friendship deepened and we exchanged countless letters and phone calls. Though we have yet to meet, our mutual dream is to one day encounter each other at the foot of the "Bust," which Sylvette herself has never seen in person.

All of which brings us back to the story of Père Angély. Near the end of 2021, while working on my research, I suddenly thought of asking Sylvette if she'd ever heard of Léon. Though she hadn't, the story fascinated her; for the challenges faced by Angély were something that she could personally identify with. Having just turned eighty-seven that November, Sylvette was losing her vision due to an advanced case of cataracts. She'd been painting all her life, but now she was forced to curtail her activity, as the complex process of oil painting was becoming increasingly difficult to manage.

Yet, she persisted. When I phoned a few days later, she was in the midst of preparing a canvas board:

"I'm painting a white board, but I'm not very inspired. Send me some nice photos!" she laughed, sounding as energetic as ever.

"I have something better; I can offer you inspiration …"

"Will you? I'd love a bit of inspiration – right now!"

"How would you like to illustrate my work on Père Angély?"

"What a lovely idea. *Oui!*"

The next morning, I received an email containing her first set of watercolors. I was delighted by her decision to take Léon and Joséphine on a walking tour of Paris and to portray them at the Place du Tertre, inspecting various canvases laid out on the cobblestones.

A few days later, she surprised me with a portrait of the collector and his child guide circling round the "Bust of Sylvette" – through a creative warp in time that allowed the blind man who was crazy for color to visit a Picasso sculpture that didn't even exist during his own lifetime.

Sylvette was far more fortunate than Léon. The following January, her eye operation was a success, and the bright colors of the world were once again within her grasp. Therefore, these paintings represent the final works composed during those twilight years, just before her ocular renaissance.

– Rob Couteau, 1 February 2022.

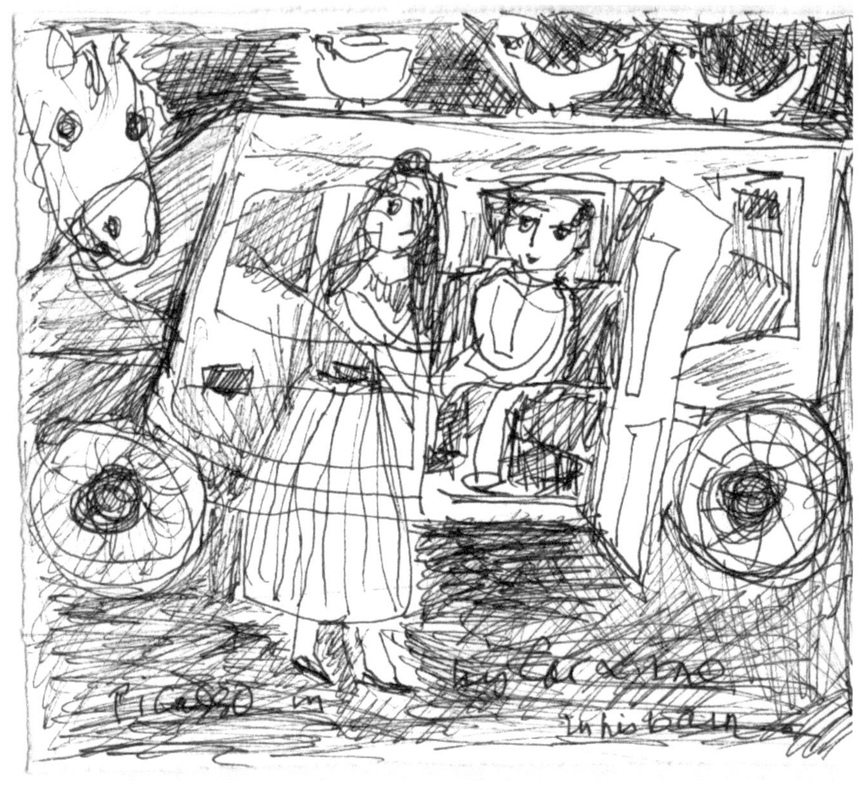

Sylvette David. *The Invitation: Picasso and Sylvette in the Hispano-Suiza*. Devon, England. December 2021. India ink on Langton watercolor paper. 7 ¼ x 8 inches.

"Picasso took me into a barn that housed his beautiful old car, his Hispano Suiza. You know, you have a chauffeur in front, and so he sat in the back and said, 'Come on in!' I'm thinking: 'Shall I go in, or not? What will he do; is he dangerous?' You know what I mean? [Laughs] Oh, that just blew my mind! It would make a very funny film! But I sat down, and he talked to me about his youth and all the things that happened to him. The poetry he wrote. And the poet who died. All these sorts of things. The circus people, *les saltimbanques*. Yes. He was extraordinary." – Sylvette David, interview with Rob Couteau, December 2017.

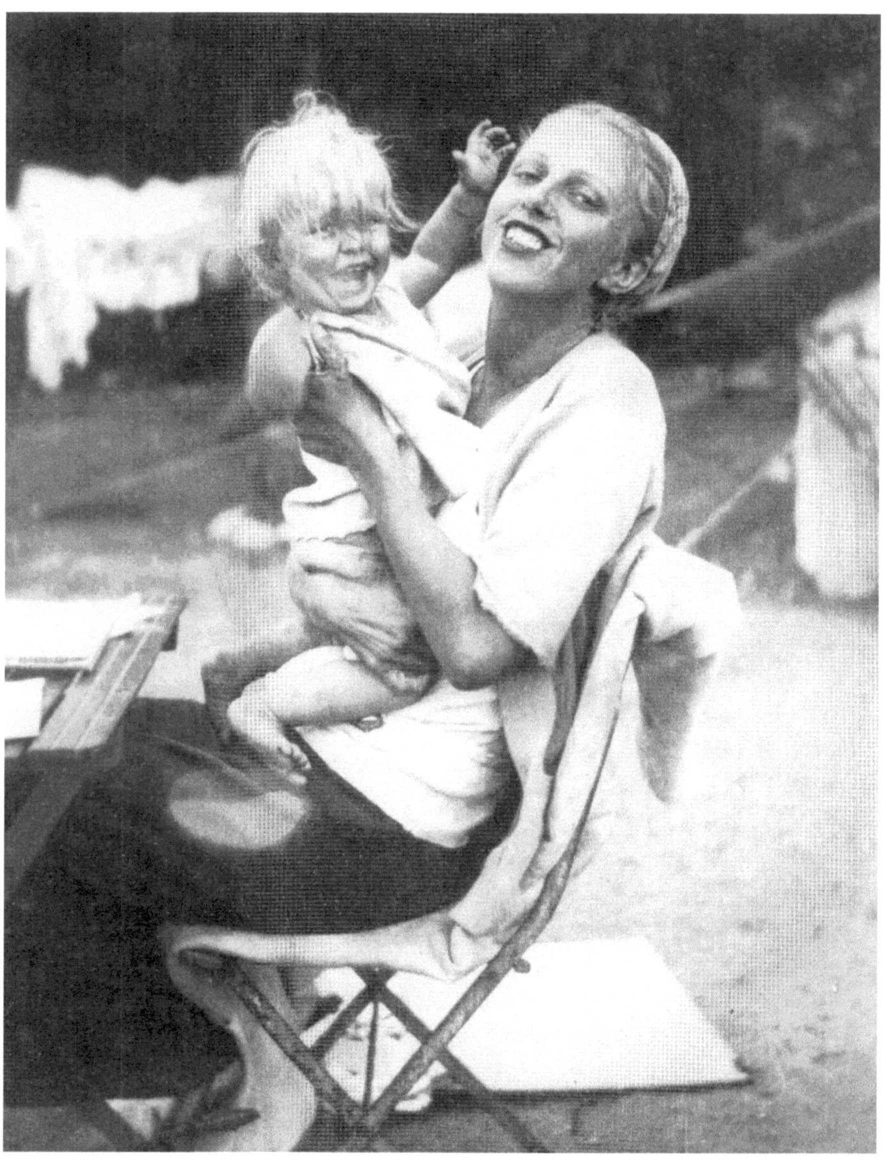

Sylvette with her mother, Honor Gell. Photo Copyright ©
Sylvette David.

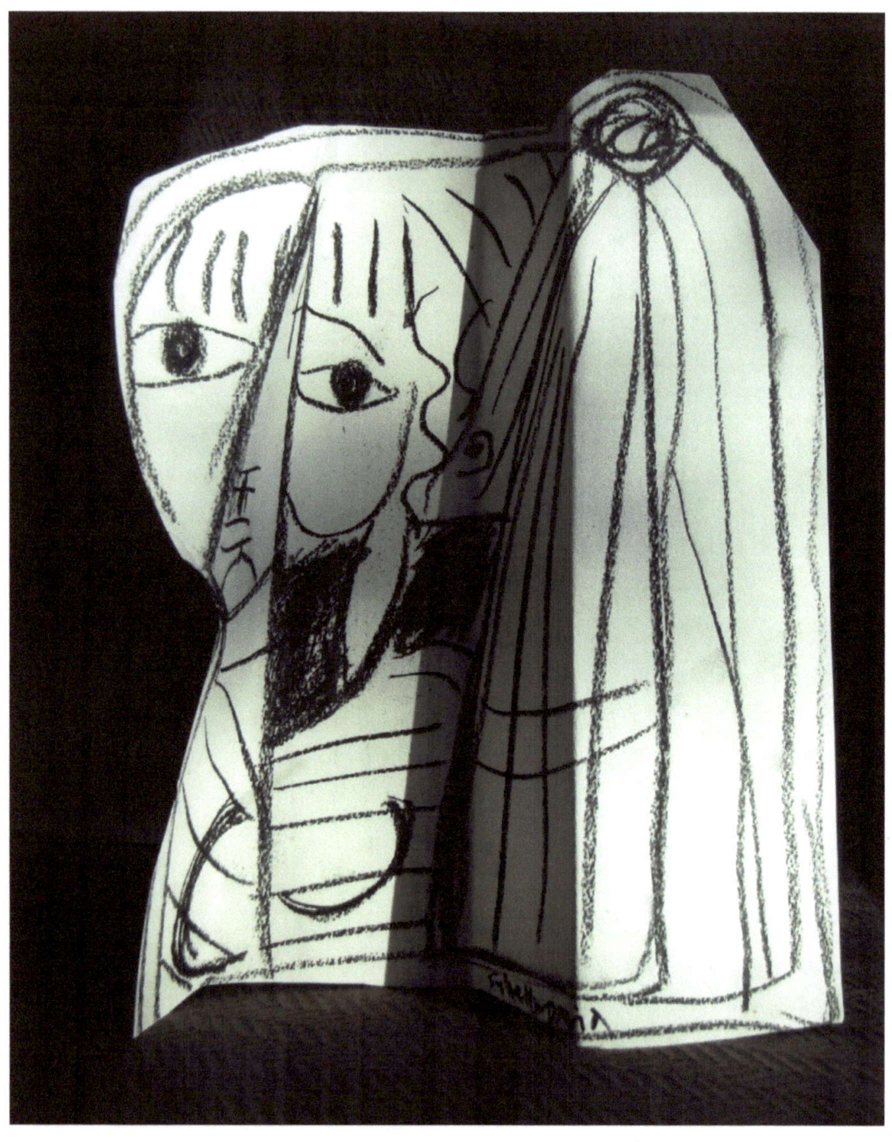

Sylvette David. *Bust of Sylvette (I)*. Devon, England. January 2021. Charcoal on folded Langton watercolor paper. 17 ¼ x 14 ¾ inches. Front view. Collection of Rob Couteau. Photo Copyright © 2022 Rob Couteau.

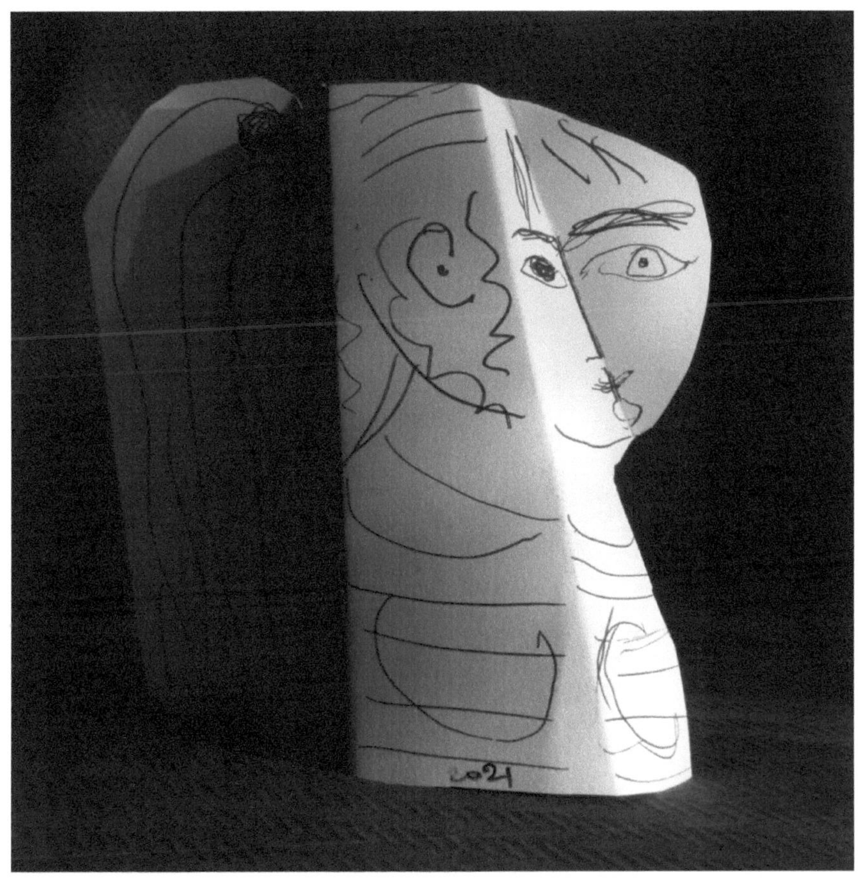

Sylvette David. *Bust of Sylvette (I)*. Rear view. Photo Copyright © 2022 Rob Couteau.

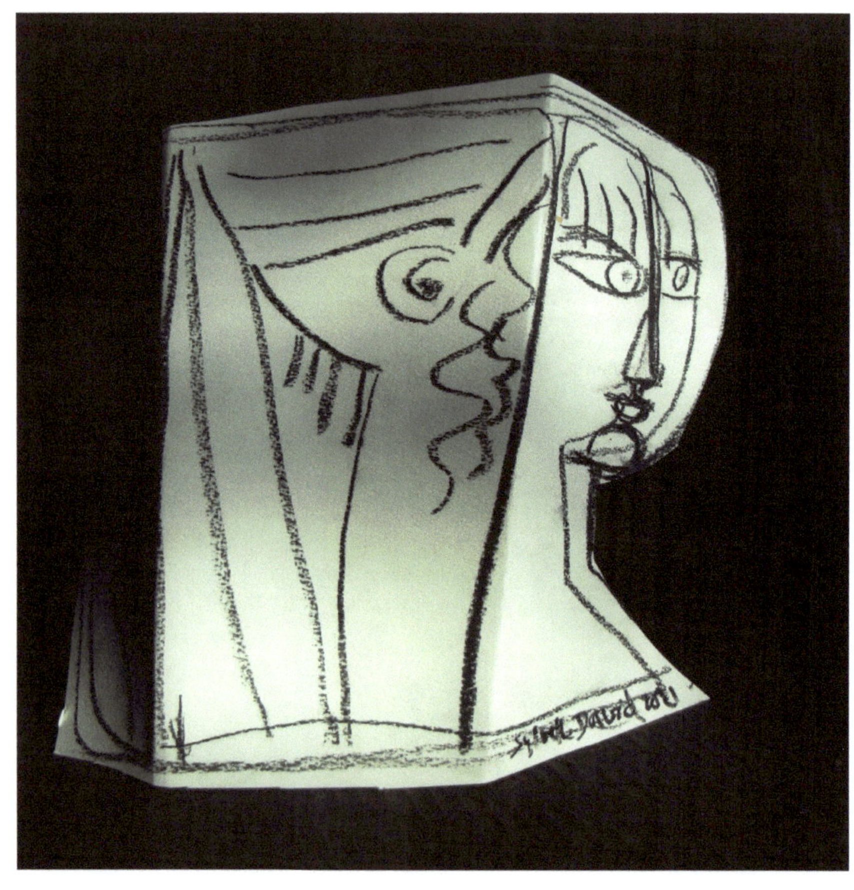

Sylvette David. *Bust of Sylvette (II)*. Devon, England. January 2021. Charcoal on folded Langton watercolor paper. 14 ¼ x 15 ¼ inches. Front view. Collection of Rob Couteau. Photo Copyright © 2022 Rob Couteau.

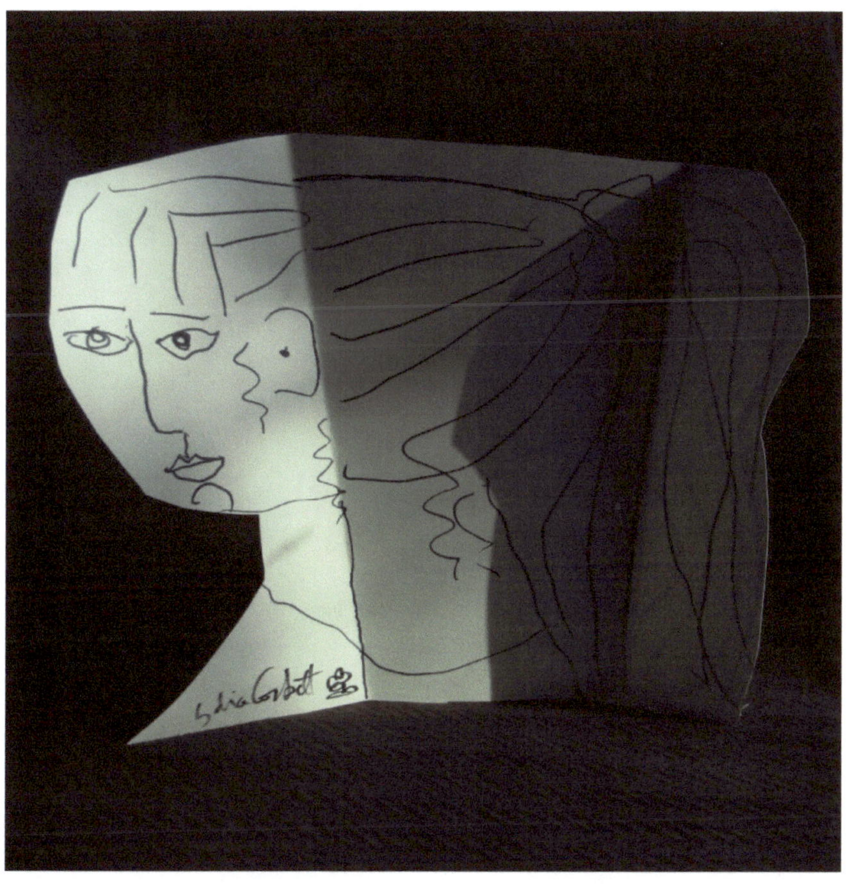

Sylvette David. *Bust of Sylvette (II)*. Rear view. Photo Copyright © 2022 Rob Couteau. After changing her name to "Lydia Corbett" in the 1960s, she now signs her work with two signatures, as both "Lydia" and "Sylvette."

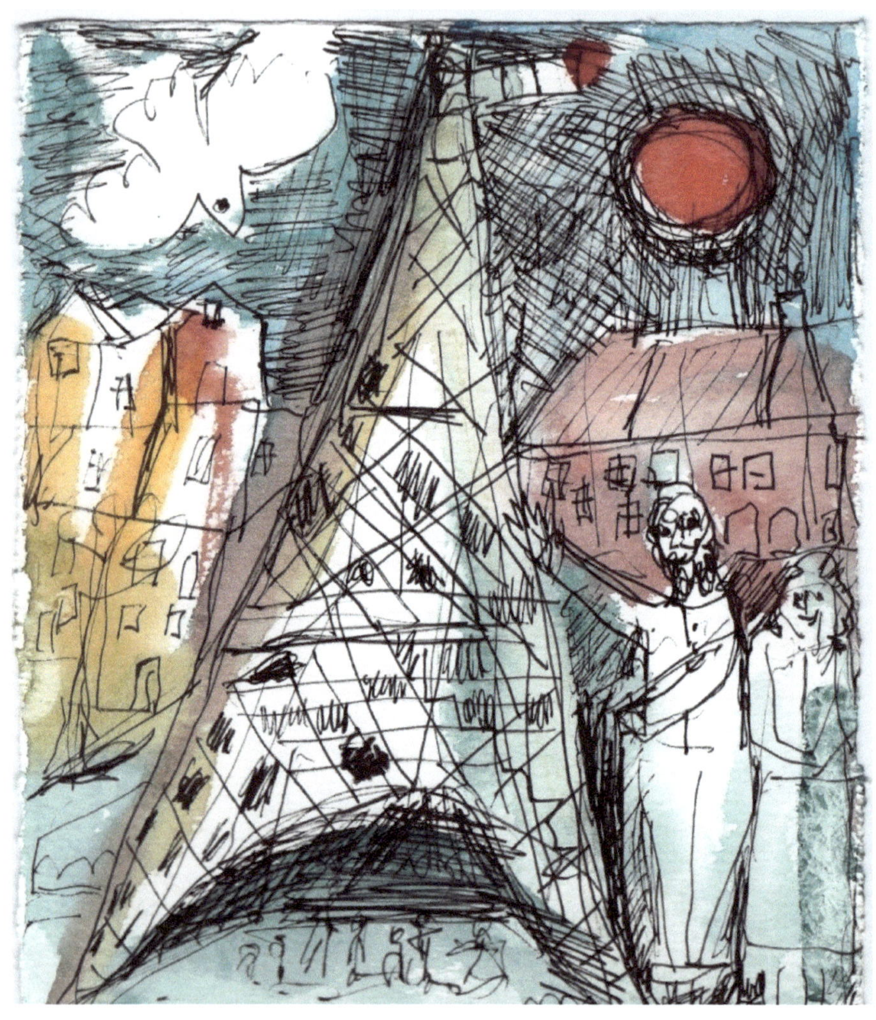

Sylvette David. *Léon Angély et Joséphine debout à la tour Eiffel.* **Devon, England. December 2021. Watercolor and India ink on Langton watercolor paper. 7 ¼ x 8 ¼ inches.**

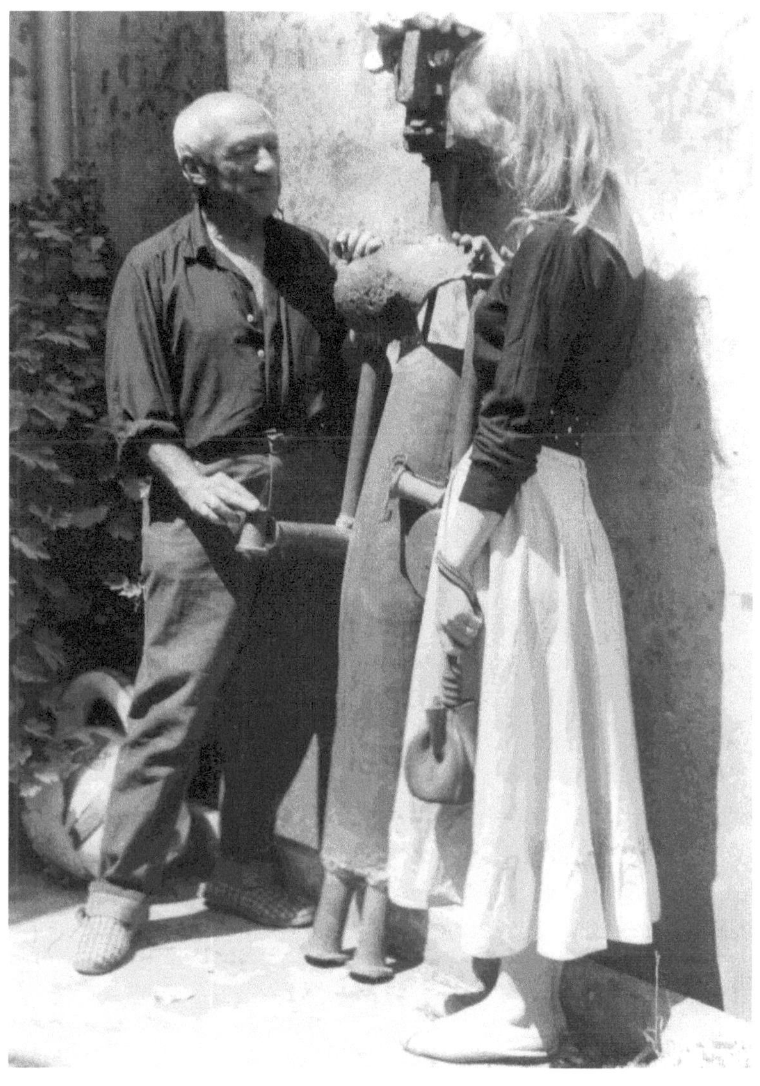

**Picasso, Sylvette, and *The Woman with the Key*. Copyright ©
1954 Toby Jellinek. "I was shut in myself, and maybe that's
why he included a key. I feel it represents me as an
awakened woman with the key to life and inner strength.
Maybe it was a message to me to become just that, to be
free. Picasso was intent on helping me open the door to my
own self-confidence."**

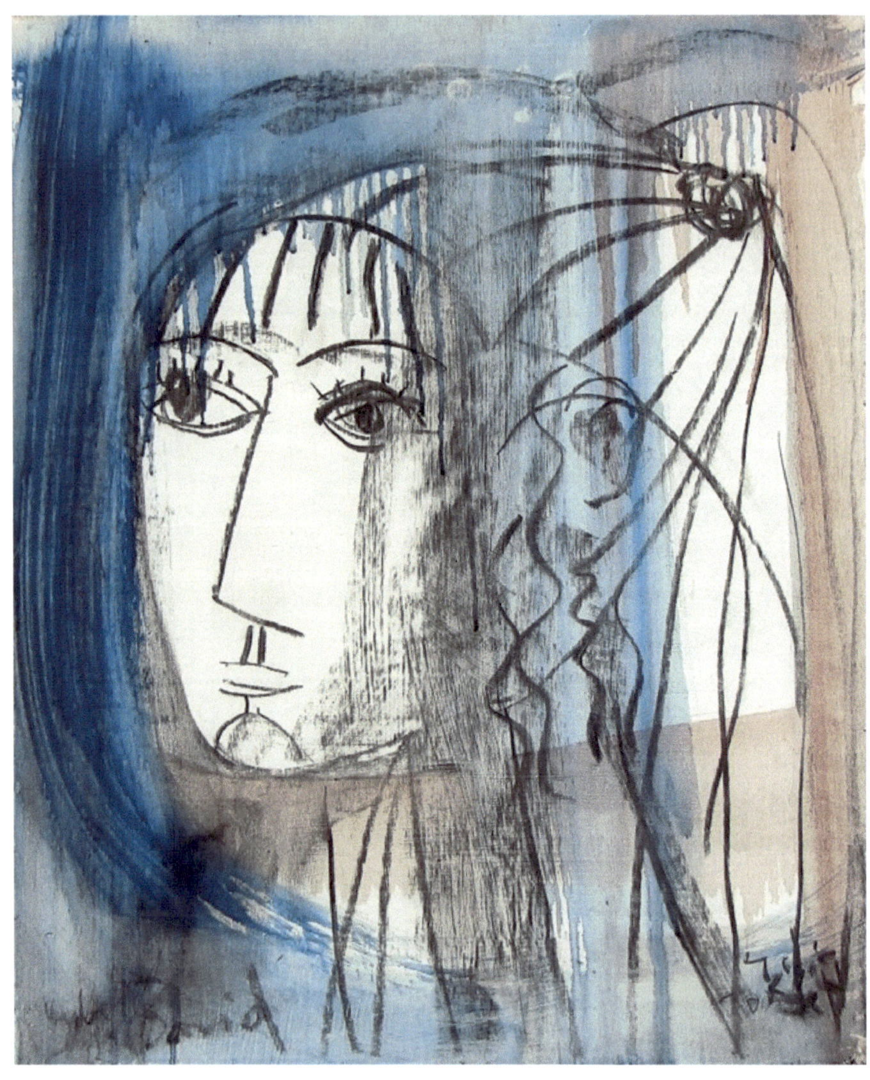

Sylvette David. *Self-portrait.* **Devon, England. 2020. Charcoal and oil on board. 20 x 16 inches. Collection of Rob Couteau. Photo Copyright © 2022 Rob Couteau.**

Bibliography

Alexandre, Paul. *The Unknown Modigliani: Drawings from the Collection of Paul Noël Alexandre.* New York: Harry N. Abrams, 1993.

Ashton, Dore. *Picasso On Art: A Selection of Views.* New York: Da Capo Press, 1988.

Bolliger, Hans. Translated by Norbert Guterman. *Picasso's Vollard Suite.* London: Thames and Hudson, 1985.

Coulton, Isabel. *I Was Sylvette: The Story of Lydia Corbett.* London: Endeavour Ltd., 2016.

Crespelle, Jean-Paul. *Modigliani: Les femmes, les amis, l'œuvre.* Paris: Presses de la Cité, 1960, e-book edition.
—Ibid. *La Vie Quotidienne à Montmartre au Temps de Picasso: 1900—1910.* Hachette litterature, 1978.

Dorgelès, Roland. *Bouquet De Bohème.* Paris, Albin Michel, 1989. (Originally published in Paris by Albin Michel, 1947.)

Douglas, Charles (aka: Charles Beadle and Douglas Goldring). *Artist Quarter: Modigliani, Montmartre and Montparnasse.* London: Pallas Athene Arts, 2018. (Originally published in London by Faber and Faber, 1941.)

Fifield, William. *Modigliani: The Biography.* New York: William Morrow and Company, 1976.

Grunenberg, Christoph, and Astrid Becker, eds. *Sylvette, Sylvette, Sylvette. Picasso and the Model*. New York: Prestel, 2014.

Laporte, Genevieve. *Sunshine at Midnight: Memories of Picasso and Cocteau*. New York: Macmillan Company, 1975.

Modigliani, Jean. *Modigliani: Man and Myth*. New York: The Orion Press, 1958.

Richardson, John. *A Life of Picasso: The Minotaur Years 1933—1943*. New York: Penguin Random House, 2021, e-book edition.

Richardson, John, and Mary McCully. *A Life Of Picasso: 1881—1906*. New York: Random House, 1991.

Salmon, André. *La Vie Passionnée de Modigliani*. Paris: Editions Gerard & Co., 1957.

Wittlin, Thaddeus. *Modigliani: Prince of Montparnasse*. New York: Bobbs Merrill, 1964.

Notes

[1] Modigliani may have borrowed this phrase from another artist. According to Paul Alexandre, "In reality these words were spoken by Henri Doucet, whose principal buyer around 1912 was an exceptionally myopic German art lover." See Paul Alexandre, *The Unknown Modigliani: Drawings from the Collection of Paul Noël Alexandre* (New York: Harry N. Abrams, 1993), p. 67. Alexandre was a close friend of Modigliani and was the subject of several of his pre-WWI paintings. He also purchased Modi's artwork, amassing a collection of over four hundred drawings. Henri Doucet (1883—1915) was a French painter.

[2] Charles Douglas (pseudonym of Charles Beadle and Douglas Goldring), *Artist Quarter: Modigliani, Montmartre & Montparnasse* (London: Pallas Athene Arts, 2018), p. 102.

[3] Beadle's presence in England during this period is documented in the diary of Aleister Crowley. According to Crowley's biographer Tobias Churton, Beadle was a dinner guest at Crowley's Chiswick, Middlesex residence five times in 1939, beginning on 6 June of that year. See Tobias Churton, *Aleister Crowley in England* (Rochester, VT: Inner Traditions, 2021), e-book edition. Regarding Beadle's date of death, his story, "Nameless Spy," which appeared in the 10 June 1947 issue of *Short Stories* magazine, "is a contemporary tale set in French North Africa and refers to the Allied Forces. It's his last known published work, and the most recent evidence of his being alive." See John Locke, "The World of Beadle," in Charles Beadle, *The Land of Ophir* (Elkhorn, CA: Off-Trail Publications, 2012), p. 2.

[4] Beadle's novel, *The Esquimau of Montparnasse* (1928), was inspired by his intimate knowledge of the bohemian scene during the 1910s and Roaring Twenties. In one passage, the "Esquimau" protagonist, seated in a café, salutes "a swarthy man in corduroys who had the features of an unwashed Roman senator." The man has "bright" eyes (from having imbibed too much alcohol and / or other intoxicants) and is identified in dialogue as "One of the few painters left in the Quarter." This is an obvious reference to Modigliani. Twenty-three years later, on page 205 of *Artists Quarter*, the narrator describes Modigliani's "charming smile, now beginning to be slightly twisted into a sneer, and the still liquid eyes

in that handsome face, resembling a Roman senator's," which "continued to fascinate women of every class."

In chapter seven of *Artist Quarter*, "The Demon of Genius," Beadle explores the influence of drugs such as opium and hashish upon the painters of the day. (Fernande Olivier also devotes a chapter to this subject, titled "Opium," in her memoir *Picasso and His Friends*.) In one of the concluding paragraphs (see page 97), the narrator includes a "personal" experience: "I have, at one time or another, experimented with every kind of dope indulged in by the artists in Montmartre and Montparnasse ..." This may have been one reason that the authors used a pseudonym.

Beadle's connection to the ex-pat *demi-monde* is also noted by biographer Neil Pearson: "Of all the pulp writers published by Obelisk, the most accomplished was Charles Beadle. Most Obelisk novels set in the alcoholic, narcotic, and sexual subcultures of the time manage, oddly, to be simultaneously daring and genteel: their authors peek at the *demi-monde* like children peeking over a fence, nervous visitors to an unfamiliar world. It was an attitude shared by most of the expatriates in Paris during the 1920s, and Charles Beadle hated them for it .... [He] had been a denizen of Montparnasse for many years before their arrival. He had known Modigliani, who died in 1920; he was an assiduous, evangelical user of opium and hashish; he was in for the long haul. He resented the presence of tourists at the orgies and drug dens he frequented, and when he encountered them he seems to have done everything he could either to corrupt them completely or to scare them away. He was contemptuous of 'morals,' dismissing them in one of his novels as mere superstitions of the majority, a majority he despised for lacking the intellectual rigor to disregard the taboos which tormented them. His voice is the most convincingly decadent on the Obelisk list, and his decadence was ideological. There was the genuine whiff of sulfur about him." Neil Pearson, *Obelisk* (Liverpool, UK: Liverpool University Press, 2007), pp. 322-24.

[5] See *Artist Quarter*, p. 224. On page 227, the narrator tells Modigliani about his experiences in Africa. Since it was Beadle and not Goldring who was known for such African expeditions, this detail provides further evidence that Beadle is the primary source for this narrative sequence.

[6] Beadle's address at 7, place du Tertre is noted as early as 18 August 1919, in *Adventure* magazine. Angély's address at 49, rue Gabrielle is inscribed on his death certificate, which I recently unearthed. (See the concluding paragraphs of this essay.)

[7] The "Bateau Lavoir" refers to a building located at 13, rue Ravignon, where Picasso lived from April 1904 to 1909. (He subsequently maintained a studio there until 1912.) "Both [Max] Jacob and [André] Salmon have been credited with inventing the nickname Bateau Lavoir (as the laundry boats moored in the Seine were called) that made this wretched building famous: Jacob, because of all the washing he saw hanging outside on his first visit; Salmon, because of its hollow boathouse resonance." John Richardson, Mary McCully, *A Life Of Picasso: 1881—1906* (New York: Random House, 1991), pp. 297-98, 309-10.

[8] Roland Dorgelès, *Bouquet De Bohème* (Paris, Albin Michel, 1989), pp. 188-89. My translation.

[9] See André Salmon, *La Vie Passionnée de Modigliani* (Paris: Editions Gerard & Co., 1957), p. 141. The quote is from the American adaptation of this chronicle. See Dorothy and Randolph Weaver, trans., *Modigliani: A Memoir* (New York: G. P. Putnam's Sons, 1961), p. 101. It's possible that Salmon mentioned Angély in his earlier Modigliani biography, *Le Vagabond de Montparnasse: vie et mort du peintre A. Modigliani* (1939), but this text is out of print and difficult to find. Goldring and Beadle quoted from it extensively and listed it as the first entry in the bibliography of *Artists Quarter*. Salmon also had the great honor of christening Picasso's groundbreaking masterpiece with its well-known title, *Les Demoiselles des Avignon*.

[10] Jean-Paul Crespelle, *Modigliani: Les femmes, les amis, l'œuvre* (Paris: Presses de la Cité, 1960), e-book edition, p. 57. My translation.

[11] Ibid., *La Vie quotidienne à Montmartre au temps de Picasso 1900—1910* (Paris: Hachette, 1978), p. 234.

[12] Jeanne Modigliani, *Modigliani: Man and Myth* (New York: The Orion Press, 1958), p. 41.

[13] While he was still in good health, Modigliani was said to compose about a hundred drawings a day. But drug and alcohol addiction soon eclipsed this prodigious output. He was later quoted as saying: "I do at least three paintings a day in my head. What's the use of spoiling canvas when nobody will buy?"

[14] Anselmo Bucci (1887 – 1955): Italian painter and printmaker, who befriended Modigliani in Paris.

[15] Thaddeus Wittlin, *Modigliani: Prince of Montparnasse* (New York: Bobbs Merrill, 1964), pp. 114-19.

[16] Orson Welles once called Mercedes McCambridge the "world's greatest living radio actress."

[17] This according to a review by R. M. Seaton, published in the Alliance, Nebraska, *Times—Herald* on 13 November 1976, p. 4.

[18] William Fifield, *Modigliani: The Biography* (New York: William Morrow and Company, 1976), p. 83. Both Fifield and Paul Alexandre render Léon's surname as "Angéli."

[19] Ibid., p. 82.

[20] By 1939, Cooper had acquired 137 cubist works.

[21] Footnoting the phrase "stupendous flair," Richardson cites as its source Crespelle's *La Vie quotidienne à Montmartre au temps de Picasso 1900—1910*, p. 230. (Crespelle's original text reads: "*un flair stupéfiant*"). John Richardson, Mary McCully, *A Life Of Picasso: 1881—1906*, pp. 351-52. Fernande Olivier was Picasso's companion during his early days in Montmartre. They began their affair during the summer of 1904, and they were living together in the Bateau Lavoir by September 1905. I could find no reference to Angély in either of Fernande's two books (*Loving Picasso* and *Picasso and His Friends*), so perhaps Richardson is relying on some other source, e.g., a French edition of her memoirs or an earlier serial publication.

[22] John Richardson, *A Life of Picasso: The Minotaur Years 1933—1943* (New York: Penguin Random House, 2021), e-book edition, p. 125.

Richardson credits Gijs van Hensbergen with first drawing a connection between Picasso and Saint Lucy. Christopher Sawyer-Lauçanno has drawn my attention to the possibility that Picasso may have been familiar with Federico García Lorca's story, "Santa Lucía y San Lázaro," which is "all about eyes." For an English-language rendition, see Sawyer-Lauçanno's translation of Lorca's *Barbarous Nights: Legends and Plays* (San Francisco: City Lights, 1991).

[23] Anna Akhmatova said of Modigliani: "He was that rarity, a painter who knew and loved poetry." Fifield goes even further and calls Modigliani "the most literary painter of the age." See William Fifield, *Modigliani*, p. 17, 33. André Salmon portrays Modigliani reciting a Dante ballad from memory, including the line: *"I' fui del cielo, e tornerovvi ancora per dar de la mia luce altrui diletto"* ("I came from heaven and shall return there once more, to delight others with my light"). See André Salmon, *Modigliani: A Memoir*, p. 102.

[24] *Blind Minotaur Being Led by a Little Girl*. 22 September 1934. Pencil on paper, 34.5 x 51.4 cm. Musée National Picasso, Paris. Ibid., p. 124.

[25] Hans Bolliger, trans. Norbert Guterman, *Picasso's Vollard Suite* (London: Thames and Hudson, 1985), p. xii. Bolliger dates the eleven Minotaur engravings from 17 May to 18 June 1933. The four blind Minotaurs were completed between 22 September and 23 October 1934.

[26] My translation. See Dore Ashton, *Picasso On Art: A Selection of Views* (New York: Da Capo Press, 1988), p. 157, citing author Dor de la Souchère, *Picasso à Antibes* (Paris: Hazen, 1960).

[27] John Richardson, *A Life of Picasso: The Minotaur Years 1933—1943*, e-book edition, p. 121.

[28] Sixth state. Paris, 23 March 1935. Etching and engraving, 49.7 x 68.8 cm. Musée National Picasso, Paris.

[29] Richardson has often remarked that the penultimate work in a Picasso "series" is usually the best; whereas the final version, although highly polished, may have crystallized into a rigid perfection, which is no longer fully energized by signs of the artist's struggle.

[30] John Richardson, *A Life of Picasso: The Minotaur Years 1933–1943*, p. 130.

[31] Ibid., p. 551, n. 11.

[32] "When he moved to Cannes in the 1950s, Picasso hung a Mithraic emblem on a studio wall. When I asked him about this sunburst ringed with spiky rays, he admitted that Mithraism fascinated him. That bulls had to be sacrificed to Mithra resonated with this lifelong lover of the corrida. He was also aware that there were connections between Christianity and Mithraism, and that some Christian festivities were said to derive from Mithraic ones." Ibid, p. 130. And Picasso's mistress Geneviève Laporte says that his bed was covered with a "white bull's hide with dark spots." See Geneviève Laporte, *Sunshine at Midnight: Memories of Picasso and Cocteau* (New York: Macmillan Company, 1975), p. 54.

[33] John Richardson, *A Life of Picasso: The Minotaur Years 1933–1943*, p. 130. An earlier version of Richardson's essay on the blind Minotaur, Père Angély, and *La Minotauromachie* appeared in the *New York Review* on 25 June 2015. Titled "Picasso's Broken Vow," it was only slightly revised when it was later featured as a passage in volume four of *A Life of Picasso*.

[34] See William Fifield, *Modigliani*, p. 83.

[35] *Etat Civil 1792–1902*, Archives de Paris; Paris, France. Accessed online via ancestry.com.

[36] According to the cemetery's interment list, Léon is buried in Division 53, line 9/52, number 208, "a gauche passage." The record indicates that the plot was purchased in 1879, when Léon was thirty-one years old. Cemetery officials later informed us that the head of the tombstone is numbered "437."

[37] When news of the planned sculpture was released to the press, Alfred H. Barr Jr., the first director of the Museum of Modern Art, was quoted in the *New York Times* as saying: "Now, in our city, we shall have a monument sprung from a two-foot high painted sheet metal, the head of

a girl with ponytail hair, as big as the head of the Giant Sphinx of Egypt." As reproduced in Sally Fairweather, *Picasso's Concrete Sculptures* (New York: Viking Penguin, 1982), pp. 114-15.

[38] The number of Picasso's Sylvette-inspired works is impossible to determine. "Friends of Picasso's, … who visited his studio in Vallauris in 1954, recalled seeing a large number of works devoted to Sylvette. Georges-Michel mentions as many as fifty portraits, some of them unfinished; [Alexander] Liberman remembered Picasso pulling some forty pencil drawings of the girl's head out of a drawer to show him. Picasso himself told Georges-Michel that he had 'made hundreds of small and large sketches' which the visitor saw lying about in the studio … Thus it is reasonable to assume that the number of pictures, or at least the number of works on paper, was originally larger than that of the surviving works and those cited in the Picasso literature today. Consequently, the series documented in the *catalogue raisonné* of Picasso's oeuvre does not begin with the first works on paper, but instead on 18 April 1954 with a very sketchy bust portrait of Sylvette." The *catalogue raisonné* contains twenty-one drawings and twenty-eight paintings of Sylvette, as well as folded-metal pieces and other sculptures. See Vera Hausdorff, "The Sylvette Series: Paintings and Drawings," in *Sylvette, Sylvette, Sylvette. Picasso and the Model*, ed. Christoph Grunenberg and Astrid Becker (New York: Prestel, 2014), p. 88.